Conflict Management For
LAW ENFORCEMENT

Non-Escalation, De-Escalation, and Crisis Intervention For Police Officers

Gary T. Klugiewicz

Dave Young

Allen Oelschlaeger

Copyright © 2018 Vistelar

All rights reserved. No part of this publication or its ancillary materials may be reproduced in any form (photocopy, digital file, audio recording) or transmitted by any means (electronic, mechanical, Internet) without prior written permission of the publisher – except as brief, referenced citations imbedded in articles or reviews.

For bulk-purchasing pricing, please contact:

Vistelar
1845 N. Farwell Ave., Suite 210
Milwaukee, WI 53202
Phone: 877-690-8230
Fax: 866-406-2374
Email: info@vistelar.com
Web: www.vistelar.com

Authors: Gary T. Klugiewicz, Dave Young and Allen Oelschlaeger

Conflict Management For Law Enforcement

ISBN-13: 978-0-9976791-8-2
ISBN-10: 0-9976791-8-2

BISAC Subject Headings:
   LAW / Ethics & Professional Responsibility
   LAW / Criminal Law / General
   PSYCHOLOGY / Education & Training

Published By Truths Publishing, Milwaukee, WI
Printed In the United States of America

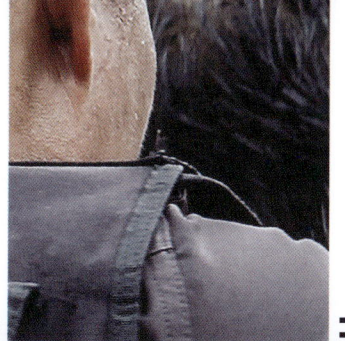

Table of Contents

Introduction 1
About This Manual
Benefits

Foundations 5
Conflict Primer
Core Principal
How To Show Respect
Practicing Empathy
The Ultimate Goal
Don't Speak Reactively

Conflict Triggers 17
Causes of Conflict
Emotional Equilibrium
Triggers of Others

6 C's of Conflict Management 23

Systemized Structure of Tactics 25

Non-Escalation 27
Review and What's Next
Framework: Context and Contact
Treat With Dignity By Showing Respect
Be Alert & Responsive; Respond, Don't React
Showtime Mindset
Proxemics 10-5-2
Universal Greeting
Listening Introduction
Beyond Active Listening

Table of Contents *continued*

De-Escalation 47
Review and What's Next
Framework: Conflict and Crisis
Redirections
Persuasion Sequence
Crisis Interventions

Ending An Interaction 63
Review and What's Next
Framework: Combat and Closure
Take Appropriate Action
Closure

Pulling It All Together 73
Review: Systemized Structure of Tactics
Point-Of-Impact Conflict Management Framework
Inconsistency Is The Enemy Of Peace
Another Strategy To Reduce Conflict
Management Is Still Required
A More Efficient Approach
Conflict Must Be Addressed Head-On
Just The Beginning

Additional Information 83
Fire Drills
Other Resources
About Vistelar
Origins of Vistelar
Acknowledgements
References and Citations

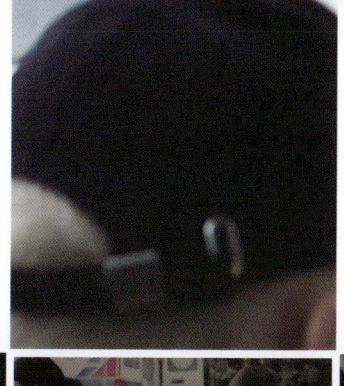

Introduction

About This Manual

This manual was developed as a resource for law enforcement professionals.

However, the principles of customer service and conflict management covered in this manual also have value to anyone within a public safety agency who would benefit from knowing how to better manage conflict with the general public, among team members, between supervisors and employees and between departments.

This is the course manual for Vistelar's *Conflict Management* in-person and online training programs for law enforcement and is a great companion to any of Vistelar's *Confidence in Conflict* books. It can also be used as a stand-alone guide for learning how to better manage conflict.

In the first part of this manual, you will learn Vistelar's core principle of conflict management, how to behave in alignment with this principle, and how to identify and develop "guards" against triggers to conflict. Also explained are Vistelar's 6 Cs of Conflict Management: *Point-Of-Impact Conflict Management Framework*™ — and its *Systemized Structure of Tactics* that make Vistelar's methodologies easy to learn, remember, apply and teach. The remainder of this manual focuses on teaching the "how-tos" of each of these tactics for providing excellent customer service and effectively managing conflict.

At the end of this manual, everything you have learned is summarized.

Whether you are reading this manual as a component of a live class or online program, in conjunction with one of our books, or in isolation from any other Vistelar training offering, we look forward to you becoming a master at conflict management.

Benefits

After reading this manual — especially if read in conjunction with another Vistelar training opportunity (e.g., live training) — you will be better prepared to respond professionally to conflict and effectively manage conflict it in both your professional and personal lives. However, our primary goal is officer safety.

You will gain the *knowledge*, *skills* and *abilities* to interact with anyone — in person, by phone or in writing — and to:

- Engage in a way to not cause conflict or unnecessarily escalate situations
- Confidently and professionally deal with questioning, anger, and verbal abuse
- Participate in difficult conversations and mediate positive outcomes
- Effectively de-escalate conflict and remain safe in crisis situations
- Persuade others to cooperate
- Know what to do and how to do it when resistance or aggression results in physical engagement
- End an interaction in a better place than where it started
- Look good on camera no matter where an interaction ends up
- If necessary, articulate a defense for taking appropriate action

GOAL

WORK ENVIRONMENT AND PERSONAL RELATIONSHIPS INCOMPATIBLE WITH VIOLENCE

The results within your agency include:

- Higher levels of citizen satisfaction[1]
- Improved team performance, morale and safety[2]
- Reduced complaints, liabilities and injuries[3]
- Protected reputation, culture and agency continuity[4]
- Reduced harm from emotional or physical violence[5]
- Decreased stress levels, lateral violence and bullying[6]
- Less compassion fatigue, absenteeism and turnover
- Not having a damaging video show up on YouTube or the evening news

Chapter 1 :: Introduction

Who Is Vistelar

Vistelar's training focuses on addressing the entire spectrum of human conflict at the point of impact — from before an interaction begins through to the consequences of how an interaction is managed.

We offer a wide range of training programs that address how to:

- Provide better customer service
- Predict, prevent and mitigate conflict
- Avert verbal and physical attacks
- De-escalate conflict
- Control crisis and aggression
- Handle physical violence

All of our training programs address the reality that, at the point of impact with a person of authority, most people ask themselves these "Four Great American Questions:" 1) Who are you? 2) Where do you get your authority? 3) Why are you here? 4) What's in it for me? – which includes these four benefits (P.O.L.E.)

- Physical Safety: improved threat assessment and physical assault avoidance
- Organizational Safety: better job performance, morale and collaboration
- Legal Safety: less risk of personal liability and looking bad on YouTube
- Emotional Safety: improved relationships, self-confidence and life quality

Our training is focused on the point of impact — the short period of time when disagreements, insults or gateway behaviors, like swearing or aggressive posturing, can escalate to conflict and on to emotional and/or physical violence, with the goal of:

- Looking good on camera
- Choreographing your response
- Communicating concern

Vistelar's training supports the best practice recommendations outlined in the International Association of Chiefs of Police (IACP) *National Consensus Policy on Use of Force*, as well as these three principles from the *Final Report of the President's Task Force on 21st Century Policing*:

- Embrace a Guardian, versus Warrior, Mindset
- Adopt Procedural Justice (emphasis on how people are treated rather than just fairness of the outcome)
- Encourage Community Engagement (support of trust-building/non-enforcement activities)

Who Is Vistelar *continued*

Vistelar's methodologies have been proven in real-world environments for over thirty years and are the subject of several books and training manuals in Vistelar's *Confidence In Conflict* series.

We offer our training via speaking engagements, workshops, and instructor schools using both live and online methods of instruction.

Our vision is to make the world safer by teaching everyone how to treat each other with dignity by showing respect.

POINT-OF-IMPACT CONFLICT MANAGEMENT TRAINING

LEARN HOW TO:

- Provide better customer service
- Predict, prevent and mitigate conflict
- Avert verbal and physical attacks
- De-escalate conflict
- Control crisis and aggression
- Handle physical violence

BENEFITS:

- Higher levels of customer satisfaction
- Reduced complaints, liabilities & injuries
- Improved team performance and morale
- Protected reputation, culture, business continuity and employee safety
- Reduced workplace violence
- Not having a damaging video show up on YouTube or the evening news

WHO WE TRAIN:

- Contact professionals who directly interact with the general public or an organization's clients
- Organizational teams who want to improve their performance by better managing conflict.

Chapter 2 :: Foundations

Foundations

Conflict Primer

Do you experience conflict in your personal life and at your work within law enforcement? Sure you do, all police officers do.

While not immediately obvious, well-managed conflict can actually result in positive outcomes. It leads to identification of problems, innovation to solve those problems and development of new skills. Without conflict, progress would come to a standstill.

Consider an officer attending a community meeting. Without conflict, no ideas to address the issues would be brought up and neighborhood problems would continue.

However, it is when conflict is poorly managed that challenges occur. Mismanaged conflict with the general public can result in complaints, liabilities and injuries. Within a law enforcement agency, it can diminish performance, morale and safety. Further, innovation stops, collaboration is stymied, turnover skyrockets and productivity drops. Within a family, it can ruin relationships, and at its worse it can result in mental health issues and suicide. And finally, if caught on camera and posted to YouTube or the evening news, poorly managed conflict can destroy reputations.

In some instances, poorly-managed conflict within organizations can even escalate to workplace violence in the form of both verbal and physical assault. Such violence can originate from customers, co-workers, personal relations, or someone with criminal intent. Workplace violence can exact a heavy emotional and physical toll on those involved, both immediately and over the long term.

In addition, poorly-managed conflict by a police officer can obviously escalate to violence in the form of both verbal and physical assault.

Conflict Management For Law Enforcement

"Peace is not absence of conflict, it is the ability to handle conflict by peaceful means."
Ronald Reagan, President of the United States (1911-2004)

One reason conflict is so prevalent is because, beyond criminal activity, it arises from disagreements, insults and gateway behaviors, like swearing or aggressive posturing, which frequently just rolls off people's backs. However, for a wide variety of reasons, things sometimes escalate.

In this program you will learn how to predict and prevent this escalation, and if necessary, de-escalate a situation by effectively managing the conflict. You will also learn how to end an interaction to achieve the best possible outcome and establish a strong foundation for the next interaction. Finally, if you struggle at all with conflict, you will gain confidence to deal with it head-on, rather than avoiding it or accommodating people by giving in just to appease them.

In summary, conflict is inevitable in law enforcement; you cannot eliminate it. However, if well managed, it drives citizen satisfaction, team performance, problem solving, innovation, collaboration and, most importantly, officer safety. If conflict is poorly managed, it can create a myriad of problems including emotional and physical injuries.

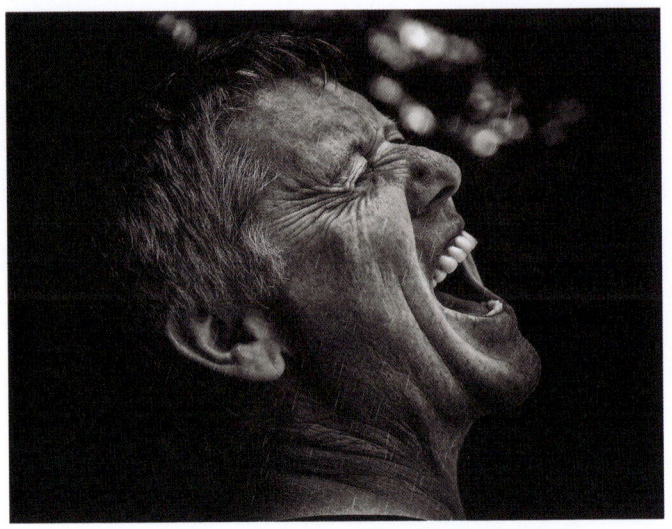

OUTCOMES OF POORLY MANAGED CONFLICT

WITHIN AN ORGANIZATION:
COMPLAINTS, LIABILITIES, AND INJURIES

WITHIN A TEAM:
DIMINISHED PERFORMANCE, MORALE, AND SAFETY

IF CAUGHT ON CAMERA:
DESTROYED REPUTATIONS

Core Principle

Let us start with the core principle of customer service and conflict management that serves as the foundation for everything we teach.

Surprisingly, many organizations are just now discovering the importance of this principle. For example, between 2013 and 2015, Google researched the role of conflict in team effectiveness. They conducted scores of interviews, observed hundreds of teams and analyzed tens of thousands of pieces of data. But, for a long time, they were stuck. Charles Duhigg, in his book Smarter, Faster, Better, quotes a person who worked on this project:

> *"We knew it was important for people to feel like they can speak up if something's wrong. But those are also the behaviors that can set people at odds. We didn't know why some groups could clash and still perform, while others would hit a period of conflict and everything would fall apart."*

After two years of work, the Google researchers concluded that all the team factors they thought would make a difference did not seem to matter at all. They could not find any correlation between team effectiveness and such factors as who was on the team, co-location of team members and use of consensus decision-making.

What they found was just one team attribute that made all the difference in team effectiveness. Teams with it performed exceptionally, and teams without it struggled.

Not surprisingly, this one attribute is identical to Vistelar's core principle of customer service and conflict management.

CORE PRINCIPLE OF CONFLICT MANAGEMENT

TREAT PEOPLE WITH DIGNITY BY SHOWING RESPECT, EVEN IF YOU DISAGREE WITH THEM

Treat people with dignity by showing respect even if you disagree with them.

We all know acknowledging people's inherent value as human beings is the right thing to do, but we also know individuals sometimes make mistakes in how they treat other people.

Dignity: our inherent value as human beings
This stands in contrast to respect, which is earned through one's actions

Why is it that we do not value dignity and always treat each other as fellow human beings? There are three reasons:

1. People do not understand that treating people with dignity, regardless of the circumstances, drives better results and is a self-serving act. Within law enforcement, if you treat everyone as human beings, you will have better relationships, improved job performance, increased work satisfaction and better field outcomes. If you treat people with dignity, they will more likely cooperate with requests, not get upset and treat you well in return.

> *"When differences divide us, treating each other with dignity by showing respect establishes the common ground for managing conflict."*
> from Vistelar's *Treat People Right* card

2. Treating people with dignity is not a natural response, especially when you disagree with them or they are treating you poorly. This type of response requires training to overcome and most people do not receive such training.

3. People do not know the well-proven specific tactics for treating people with dignity.

Please Note ...

"The Google experience points to the face that conflict is inevitable in all professions. What's different between professions are the established rules of engagement. Within law enforcement, treating people with dignity is good for results and good for the officer but, like Google discovered, it is hard to teach. Law enforcement officers deal with many situations where people are at their worst. Over time, just to keep sane, officers become desensitized, which creates a 'he/she doesn't deserve to be treated well' mentality. We need to constantly remind ourselves that treating people with dignity is good for results and good for the officer."

Kevin Shults, Major, Broward County Sheriff's Office, Florida

In this manual, you will continue to be reminded of the importance of treating people with dignity to drive better results and you will be taught how to overcome your natural reactions to disagreements and being treated poorly. More importantly, you will learn the specific tactics for how to treat people with dignity, especially difficult people. That is the primary focus of this program.

The first thing to know about how to treat people with dignity is that, in order to do so, you must show them respect.

This does not mean that you need to respect everyone. That would be impossible since respect is based on your personal values and must be earned. However, it is essential that you show everyone respect. All people deserve to be shown respect.

How To Show Respect

Diversity education teaches the proper way to treat people of different backgrounds, races and genders. This can be challenging given the subtleties of cross-cultural expectations.

To be effective at customer service and conflict management, you must realize how ALL people want to be treated, regardless of their race, religion, gender, sexual orientation, culture, etc.

All people want to be shown respect and here are the five approaches for doing this:

1. See world through their eyes
2. Listen with all senses
3. Ask and explain why
4. Offer options, let them choose
5. Give opportunity to reconsider

These five approaches describe how all people want to be treated. Everyone wants to be shown empathy, listened to, asked to do something rather than being told, provided an explanation for why they are being asked, offered options to choose from, and given an opportunity to rethink a decision.

Here is a further explanation of each of the five approaches to showing people respect.

1. See World Through Their Eyes

Showing empathy, which is taking another person's perspective, enables you to treat that person the way you would want to be treated if you were him or her and in the exact same circumstances. Doing this with everyone produces better outcomes.

Example: "You must be worried about your friend," and then pause and truly listen to what he or she might have to say.

2. Listen With All Senses

The most powerful way to show respect to human beings is to listen to them, which is a much different practice than just hearing them. You hear raindrops, but to truly listen to people you must use all your senses. Besides just hearing the other person's words and tone of voice, be attentive to visual cues like facial expression, eye contact, posture and body language — as well as smell (been drinking?), touch (tense?) and taste (smoker?) cues.

Example: Listen to a citizen's concerns about your agency, rather than just hearing his or her words while you're formulating a response in your head.

3. Ask and Explain Why

Every time you would like someone to do something, make a conscious effort to ask him or her to do it rather than tell them. Show people respect by asking a question rather than barking a command. Asking is for human beings, telling is for dogs (sit, roll over, bark).

Then, once you have asked, make the assumption that people can be easily confused. Presume the individuals with whom you interact may not understand what is going on or have any idea what will happen next. Take the time to provide an explanation for why things are done as they are.

Realize that, if you don't explain why, the other person will likely fill in the blanks with their own reasons which could be incorrect and will probably be negative.

How To Show People Respect

- See world through their eyes
- Listen with all senses
- Ask and explain why
- Offer options, let them choose
- Give opportunity to reconsider

Ask Example: "Can you please come with me?" rather than the command "Come with me!"

Explain Why Example: "The reason I stopped you is because I recorded you driving eighty miles per hour when the posted speed limit is sixty."

4. Offer Options, Let Them Choose

People want to feel empowered to make their own decisions even when there are tight restrictions on their behavior. Look for ways to give people a couple of options from which to choose, rather than a single choice you have selected for them.

Example: "You can give me your license and make it to your son's soccer game on time or, if you refuse, this is going to take much longer. Can you work with me here?"

5. Give Opportunity To Reconsider

People sometimes make mistakes. In the heat of the moment, they might make a rude comment or refuse a request. If there is no safety concern, allow them to save face and give them another chance.

Example: "Is there anything I can say to help you change your mind. I would hope so."

You may already be applying these five approaches for showing people respect in many of your interactions. However, remember the goal: to show respect to EVERYONE with whom you interact, ALL THE TIME.

Why? Because at the end of the day, doing so drives better results and is a self-serving act.

Practicing Empathy

Empathy is taking another person's perspective. It is the engine that drives the effectiveness of all Vistelar customer service and conflict management tactics.

Empathy should not be confused with sympathy, which is a feeling of sorrow for another person's misfortune. To be effective at customer service and conflict management, there is no need or advantage to share in the sorrow and distress of others. Why? Because it can:

- Distract you from the task at hand
- Cloud your judgment in dealing with the conflict
- Affect your personal life

How do you practice *Empathy* with another person? By applying the *Empathy Triad*:

1. Acknowledge the other person's perspective. This first element of the *Empathy Triad* can be used when interacting with someone for the first time. In such situations, you know little about the other person so taking his or her perspective is difficult.

    Whatever the other person might say, you can respond with statements like: "Thank you for sharing that with me." — "Hmm, I never thought of it that way." — "Huh, that's interesting."

2. Seek to understand the other person. Try to understand his or her perspective so you can treat the individual the way you would want to be treated if you were that person and in the exact same circumstances.

    By listening to another person with all your senses, you can learn his or her needs, wants and desires (active intelligence gathering) and then, based on this newfound knowledge, treat the person the way you think he or she wants to be treated.

3. Anticipate the other person's needs. Consider what that person will be thinking or feeling immediately following the interaction, the next day or later. The goal is to treat the other person the way that person may not even know he or she wants to be treated.

    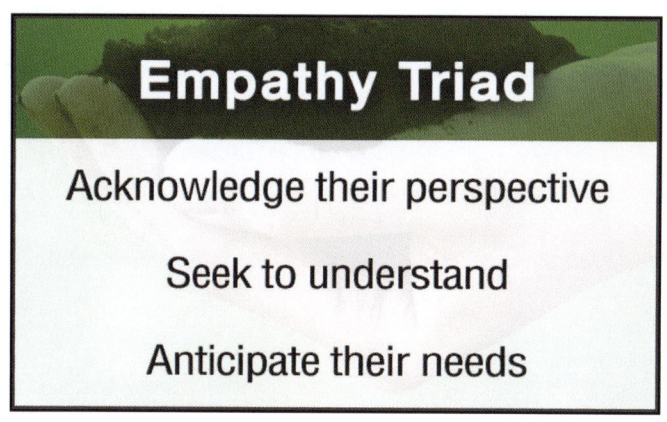

    Having the capacity to practice this third element of the *Empathy Triad* is the "secret sauce" of customer service and conflict management.

Empathy is NOT sympathy. Nor is it agreeing with or respecting the thoughts or actions of another person.

Instead, *Empathy* is a professional approach for communicating concern and active intelligence gathering about where the other person is coming from. These are both essential components for providing excellent customer service and effectively managing a conflict situation.

> ### Empathy Can Be Uncomfortable
>
> Practicing empathy can be uncomfortable. For example, the response to a mother abusing her own child would be condemnation of the mother by almost everyone. However, that is not practicing empathy. An empathetic response would be to try to put yourself in the mother's shoes; to try to see the world through the mother's eyes. For most people, that would be uncomfortable, even painful, so they do not try. However, practicing empathy is a learned skill, at which you can only improve by trying. So, view that uncomfortable feeling as a challenge. Push through it and you will improve your ability to perform this valuable skill.

Empathy is often described as the golden rule: "Do unto others as you would have them do unto you." However, that is not an accurate description because it suggests treating others based on your perspective, rather than their perspective.

A better description of *Empathy* is: "Do unto others as you would have them do unto you, if you were them and were in the exact same circumstances."

That is *Empathy* — seeing the world through the other person's eyes instead of yours; understanding the other person's perspective.

Again, *Empathy* is the engine that drives the effectiveness of all Vistelar customer service and conflict management tactics. It enables "active intelligence gathering," which drives increased understanding of the other person so you can be more effective at managing conflict and delivering exceptional customer service.

> ### A Citizen Example
>
> Let us look at an example to see an application of the *Empathy Triad*.
>
> Imagine you are a citizen and you walk into a police department after having your car stolen.
>
> You are tired, angry and do not know anything about stolen cars. The officer on duty has dealt with many stolen vehicles, and if she were in your situation, would probably just want to be left alone to investigate the theft on her own. However, that may not be how you want to be treated.
>
> If she is a good officer she will acknowledge you are upset because someone stole your car, acknowledging your perspective. Then, she will try to seek to understand you and your situation so she can see the problem through your eyes. During this process she will discover you know little about how to protect your car from having it stolen.
>
> Her goal should be to fully and accurately understand your needs, wants and desires so she can treat you the way you want to be treated. That requires *Empathy*.
>
> Now imagine the officer did a good job and you left the police department in your car because it was recovered while you were talking to the officer. You are a happy customer — right?

> ### A Citizen Example *continued*
>
> Possibly — but possibly not, because the officer did not practice the third element of the *Empathy Triad*. She did not consider what you would be thinking or feeling immediately following the interaction, the next day or later, and therefore, did not adequately anticipate your needs.
>
> As a result, there is a high likelihood that after getting back home, you would be dissatisfied with her service. Here is why: she didn't offer you what you need to prevent your car from being stolen in the future: advice about ignition locking devices, alarms, clubs or whatever.
>
> To summarize:
>
> - A good officer would treat you with dignity by showing respect.
> - A better officer would, first, acknowledge your perspective (you are upset because someone stole your car) and then try to seek to understand your needs, wants and desires, so she could treat you the way you want to be treated.
> - An outstanding officer would anticipate your needs (you never want your car stolen again) and offer you advice on how to protect your car from being stolen.
>
> This individual, by all rights, was a good officer but not an outstanding one because she failed to practice the third element of the *Empathy Triad*. She was probably kicking herself that night for not suggesting a solution to what you were most upset about — having your car stolen and not wanting that to ever happen again.

The Ultimate Goal — Establish A Social Contract

By *Showing Respect*, practicing *Empathy* and applying the conflict management tactics you will learn in this manual, the *Ultimate Goal* of Vistelar's training is to establish a professional *Social Contract* within your agency for how people are to be treated — a voluntary agreement by all employees to consistently treat everyone with dignity by showing respect.

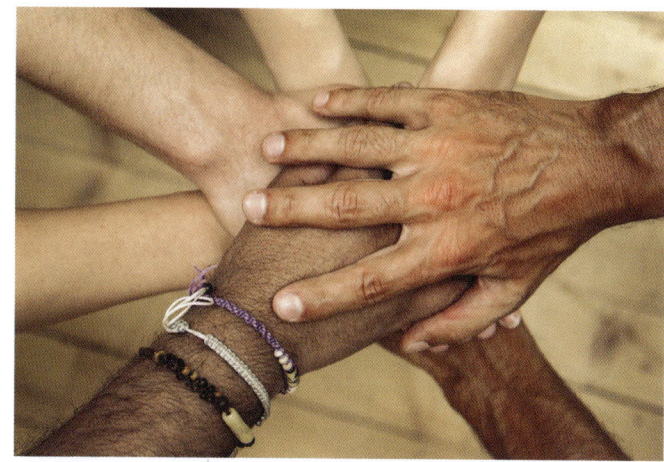

A well-established professional *Social Contract* creates an environment that promotes cooperation, performance excellence and safety, and that is incompatible with emotional and physical violence.

An example of a social contract exists in most libraries, where there is a voluntary agreement to be quiet. It does not matter if you are a business executive, the janitor, or an ex con. If you are making too much noise, the rest of the library patrons know it is OK to "shush" you, and they will do so without hesitation. Then, if that does not work, the library's social contract makes it acceptable for the library staff to get involved and if necessary, request the help of a security officer or the police.

Other social contracts with which you may be familiar exist in banks and places of worship.

For a professional *Social Contract* to be established, there must be clear expectations for how people should be treated and consistent enforcement of those expectations.

The *Ultimate Goal* of this program is to establish such a *Social Contract* within your agency. If someone – whether it is a citizen or an employee – is being treated poorly, then everyone within the agency is empowered to take the appropriate action. For example, an officer may say something like, "What is going on here? That's not how we treat people around here."

"Inappropriate behavior that goes uncorrected becomes the social norm"

Joel Lashley, author of *Confidence In Conflict For Healthcare Professionals*

Only when a professional *Social Contract* for how people are treated is established within a law enforcement agency can *The Ultimate Goal* of this training to be fully realized.

> **Please Note …**
>
> A social contract can also support negative behaviors. We all know of organizations that effectively have a voluntary agreement among employees to act in ways that promote conflict. In such organizations, the journey towards a dignity-driven social contract will obviously take longer.

The positive internal outcomes of establishing a professional *Social Contract* concerning how people are treated can take some time.

Interactions by an agency's police officers with the public generally begin and end quickly; therefore the results, such as increased citizens satisfaction, cooperation with directions and less injuries, are seen immediately.

SOCIAL CONTRACT
VOLUNTARY AGREEMENT BY ALL EMPLOYEES TO CONSISTENTLY TREAT EVERYONE WITH DIGNITY BY SHOWING RESPECT

In contrast, within the internal operations of an agency, the outcomes of everyone interacting the right way at the point of impact — at meetings, in one-on-one discussions, in the hallway, at lunch, or within teams — takes time to be realized. Each individual interaction has a positive short-term result, but the agency impact, such as increased performance, higher morale, more innovation and lower turnover, is a longer-term proposition.

When effective conflict management is utilized within a law enforcement agency, arguments go from being destructive to productive: people more openly share ideas, conflicts stop being allowed to fester and instead, get resolved, and team efficiency and productivity go up. But, again, all this takes time to be realized.

As a law enforcement professional you will see the positive results of better conflict management right away in your day-to-day interactions, but to gain the full benefits of developing a professional *Social Contract*, you will need to have some patience. It will be worth the wait.

Chapter 2 :: Foundations

Expectation Contracting

At the beginning of Vistelar's instructor-led programs, we go through a process of "expectation contracting" among the instructors and students — with everyone signing onto this agreement:

"We will treat each other with dignity by showing respect, even if we disagree."

The goal of this activity is to start the process of developing a professional *Social Contract* within class.

Over the last 30+ years we have discovered that, for students to learn best, the classroom must be an emotionally and physically safe environment, so that everyone:

- Actively participates without hesitation
- Feels listened to and supported as they share their opinions and attempt new skills
- Offers and accepts supportive feedback

Within a law enforcement agency, expectation contracting, usually initiated by the chief, is the first step on the journey towards establishing a professional *Social Contract*. Once everyone understands the chief's expectations, the next step is for individuals to set an example — "I'm going to treat you with dignity by showing you respect. I ask the same from you".

Then the goal should be to have a majority of the officers setting that example. When that happens, you are well on your way to having a professional *Social Contract* for how people are treated embedded in your agency.

Don't Speak Reactively

When interacting with others who are acting badly, especially when negative emotions are being triggered, do not reactively blurt out what first pops into your mind. There are three reasons for this:

1. In the heat of the moment, what you reactively say could unnecessarily escalate a situation. Or, you may make comment you regret or that results in a citizen complaint. As you have probably experienced, people rarely make good decisions when they are angry or frustrated.

2. What you reactively say could be based on ineffective methods or advice you have learned over time from friends, family members or colleagues, such as:

    - Ignore their bad behavior
    - Kill them with kindness
    - If you say something, you will make things worse
    - Defend your ego and save face

Rather than improving a situation, these methods will usually empower a badly-behaving individual to escalate his or her actions.

> 3. If you speak reactively, you might perform well in one situation and poorly in another, because your natural reactions are not grounded in proven principles. You could be naturally skilled in interacting with others, but because you do not fully understand how and why you do what you do, you may sometimes make mistakes — especially if you are having a bad day. In addition, you will likely struggle to teach others how you do what you do.

BE CONSISTENT IN HOW YOU TREAT PEOPLE

Such inconsistency in addressing bad behavior causes the same problems within an organization that parents discover in dealing with children; it leads to more bad behavior. By not speaking reactively, and instead, basing your response on the training in this manual, you will be more consistent in how you treat people.

When interacting with others who are acting badly, don't speak reactively. Instead, consciously pause and then apply the tactics you are learning in this manual.

Please Note ...

Don't Speak Reactively is about what words you use in the heat of the moment. Just saying what naturally pops into your mind (reacting) is almost never the right approach. Instead, you should take a deep breath and thoughtfully respond (see *Be Alert & Decisive*; *Respond, Don't React* and *Showtime Mindset*).

However, "winging it" can work when protecting your personal safety. When out in the world, you should trust your instincts and do not ignore behaviors that give you feelings of uneasiness. If you feel unsafe, be decisive and take the appropriate action to maintain your safety.

Chapter 3 :: Conflict Triggers

Conflict Triggers

Causes of Conflict

Here is a quick summary of what has been covered so far:

- Core Principle: Treat people with dignity by showing respect
- How To Show Respect: Five approaches: see world through their eyes; listen with all senses; ask and explain why; offer options, let them choose; give opportunity to reconsider
- Empathy: Engine that drives the effectiveness of all Vistelar customer service and conflict management tactics, via the *Empathy Triad*
- Social Contract: voluntary agreement by all employees to consistently treat everyone with dignity by showing respect

These are the *Foundations* of effective conflict management.

In this section you will learn the causes of conflict and how to keep it from erupting in you and in others.

Conflict occurs when disagreements or insults escalate, rather than just rolling off a person's back. Why does this happen? Why do differences and slights sometimes affect you negatively and other times don't?

The reason is the presence or absence of *Conflict Triggers*, which can come in the form of spoken words, tone of voice, facial expressions, hand position, body language, posture and physical positioning. When these triggers are present, an interaction that might otherwise be considered routine can escalate to conflict.

There are two main forms of *Conflict Triggers*:

1. Universal triggers, which cause conflict in almost everyone, such as:

- Indignity — from violations to a person's intrinsic value as a human being, such as insults, humiliation or most any action based on prejudice or explicit/implicit bias, which can provoke retaliation or revenge.

    When someone's dignity is violated, the natural reaction is to retaliate or seek revenge. This response is just baked into our DNA because such violations threaten the very essence of who we are, and as you have likely experienced, often remain in our memories forever. Being treated with indignity can cut deeper and fester longer than any physical injury.

- Fear — from emotional or physical threats, often resulting from prejudices, such as gender, race/ethnicity, religion, social class, politics, ideologies, age, disability, sexuality, language, nationality, occupation, education, criminality and physical appearance.

- Stress — from work demands, relationship difficulties, financial problems, emotional disturbances, pain, mental disorders, or being under the influence of drugs or alcohol, which can cause emotional fragility.

    CONFLICT TRIGGERS
    - **UNIVERSAL**
    - **PERSONAL HOT BUTTONS**

- Vulnerability — from being viewed as lower in status than others, which can lead to becoming the target of bullying, verbal abuse and threats.

2. Personal triggers, which are unique to you; think of these as your personal hot buttons, such as:
    - Name calling, derogatory remarks
    - Sarcastic tone, dismissive behaviors
    - Eye rolling, inappropriate smiling or laughing
    - Intimidating postures, finger pointing

Please Note ...

Prejudice and bias, whether implicit or explicit, can be a factor within each conflict trigger. Sometimes our prejudices and biases come through (even subconsciously) in your facial expressions, hand position or tone of voice.

For example, if you have a negative bias towards a specific group of people, your feelings towards them may be inadvertently displayed to others through an eye roll or hand gesture. Furthermore, it could seep into your communication via a sarcastic tone.

Chapter 3 :: Conflict Triggers

> **Please Note ... *continued***
>
> If you apply the core philosophy of this training (show people respect even if you disagree with them) to everyone with whom you interact, your prejudices will be invisible. That invisibility will make it infinitely easier to be effective at conflict management.
>
> *"Prejudice is a great time saver. You can form opinions without having to get the facts."*
>
> E. B. White, American writer (1899 - 1985)

Conflict Triggers cause people to be more susceptible to conflict, so it is important for you to be aware of yours. With that awareness as a starting point, you can learn how to minimize their impact on you.

Note: societal issues, such as drug abuse, gangs, poverty and poor family functioning, are other *Conflict Triggers*, but are beyond the scope of this training program.

Emotional Equilibrium

When one or more of your *Conflict Triggers* are present in an interaction, your goal should be to minimize their impact on you, so you can keep your cool rather than allowing your reactions to cause a situation to escalate. This is called maintaining your *Emotional Equilibrium*.

Two methods to maintain your *Emotional Equilibrium* are to:

1. Consider that your behavior is likely being caught on camera and, even if it is not, you are always in the public eye.

   With street cameras, body cameras, smart phone cameras and hidden cameras, your "reaction" could end up on YouTube, the evening news, or any social media channel for the whole world to see and forever remember.

   Entire professions are now facing this challenge. For example, as you well know, videos of law enforcement incidents are in the news almost every day. Internet and news media do not cover the millions of good police interactions but will broadcast anything bad that happens.

2. Consider the situation of the other person — practice *Empathy*

   Put yourself in the other person's shoes. Is it possible he or she is activating your personal triggers inadvertently or as a response to something else going on in his or her life? When *Empathy* is deeply practiced, being angry with anyone becomes quite difficult.

Either of these two considerations should have a calming effect on your emotions.

Another effective way to maintain your *Emotional Equilibrium* is to build *Trigger Guards*. Here is how:

a. Define them — as stated previously, be aware of your *Conflict Triggers*

b. Name them — label your *Conflict Triggers*, so you can acknowledge them.

   For example, as a police officer you might have a *Conflict Trigger* of being asked, "Want a donut?" – so he would label that trigger as "Mr. Donut."

c. Own them — take responsibility for how you respond to *Conflict Triggers*

   For example, when faced with a "Want-a-donut" question, you would say to yourself, "Ah, another Mr. Donut" and move on, rather than taking it personally.

Building *Trigger Guards* creates an internal warning system to alert you when you are in danger of allowing your *Emotional Equilibrium* to become disrupted so you can pause and thoughtfully respond rather than impulsively react.

An additional method to maintain your *Emotional Equilibrium* is to consider whom you represent, such as your family, coworkers, employer, community, or even the entire law enforcement profession.

Despite how you might feel inside, your goal should be to keep your ego out of the situation and not show a negative reaction.

You are in control of how you respond to the behavior of others. Be aware of your *Conflict Triggers* and take personal responsibility for them, with the goal of maintaining your *Emotional Equilibrium*.

MAINTAIN YOUR EMOTIONAL EQUILIBRIUM

- REALIZE YOU'RE LIKELY BEING RECORDED
- PRACTICE EMPATHY
- BUILD TRIGGER GUARDS
- CONSIDER WHO YOU REPRESENT

Triggers of Others

Now that you are aware of your *Conflict Triggers* and know how to maintain your *Emotional Equilibrium*, realize that others have *Conflict Triggers* of their own.

To prevent conflict — with citizens, other officers, your supervisor, friends, family or whoever — you must be careful your spoken words, tone of voice, facial expressions, hand position, body language, posture or physical positioning do not set off the *Conflict Triggers* of others.

Chapter 3 :: Conflict Triggers

Reflect on your own *Conflict Triggers* and consider these additional possibilities:
- Use of profanities
- Facial expressions that could be interpreted as disapproval
- Body postures that may communicate superiority
- Pointing of the "parental" finger
- Lecturing in an authoritarian manner
- Ordering, moralizing, blaming, shaming, arguing, criticizing, lying
- Use of a sarcastic or condescending tone of voice
- Veiled or explicit threats
- Eye rolling or sighing
- Any indication of prejudice
- Any violations of a person's dignity

If a situation requires you to assert yourself, such as to get your needs met or to address a violation of your dignity, use "I statements" instead of "You statements" that may come across as blaming or judgmental.

If a situation requires you to assert yourself, such as to get your needs met or to address a violation of your dignity, use "I statements" instead of "You statements" that may come across as blaming or judgmental.

You statement: "You are rude to cut in in line"

I statement: "I believe I was next in line"

In your "I statements," avoid using:
- Inflammatory words, such as fail, neglect, ignore — always, never, constantly — frequently, often, repeatedly
- Victim words, such as hurt, disappointed or let down
- Explanations as to why you need to assert yourself — keep your comments focused on the other person's behavior
- Exaggerations of the impact of the other person's behavior on you
- Excessive repetition — assert yourself confidently one or two times to let your feelings be known and then move on

In addition, realize there are some things you should just never say because most people will react negatively. Here are some examples of what not to say, with an alternative in parentheses:
- "Calm down" (alternative: "Can you explain what's happening?")
- "I know just how you must feel" (alternative: "I want to help you any way I can")
- "I need you to do this for me" (alternative: "Would you please")

- "What is your problem?" (alternative: "What can I do to help?")
- "You people" (alternative: "Will everyone please …")

You can prevent a lot of conflict by being careful to not set off the *Conflict Triggers* of individuals with whom you interact. Realize that most others have not likely been trained on how to maintain their *Emotional Equilibrium*.

> **Rewind Button**
>
> In managing conflict with another person, be aware that each person has his or her own personal conflict triggers that you may set off. If you inadvertently activate someone's trigger, the simplest and best response is to apologize and ask to start over. We call this pushing the *Rewind Button*.
>
> If you clearly do something wrong, do not hesitate to apologize. As a contact professional, you are not apologizing for doing your job; you are simply acknowledging and expressing regret for your mistake. Making an apology does not weaken your authority — in fact, it makes you appear stronger by showing you are not afraid to be human and consider the feelings of others.

TRIGGERS OF OTHERS
- **BODY LANGUAGE**
- **PHYSICAL POSITIONING**
- **HAND PLACEMENT**
- **POSTURE**
- **FACIAL EXPRESSIONS**
- **TONE OF VOICE**
- **SPOKEN WORDS**

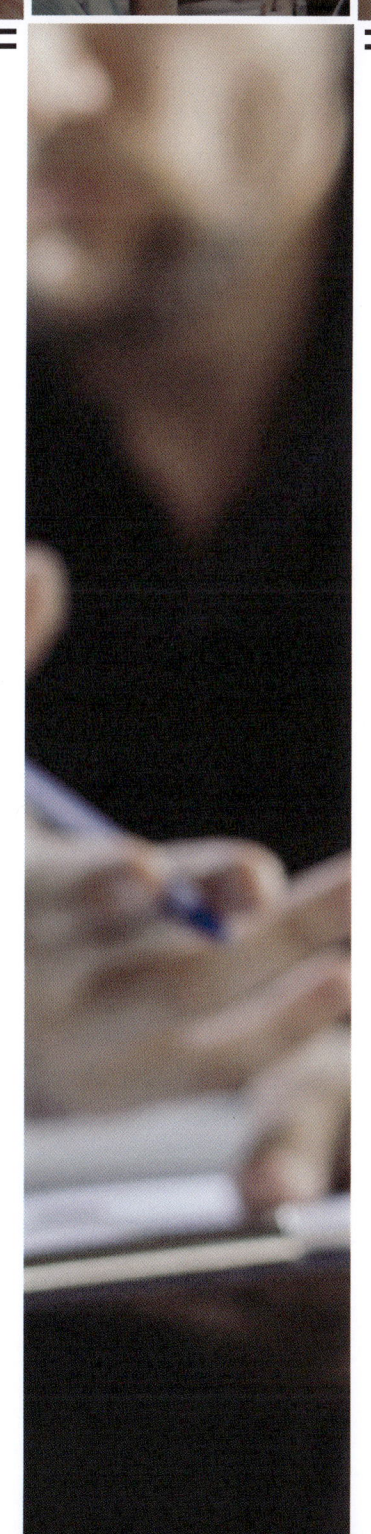

Chapter 4 :: 6 C's of Conflict Management

6 C's of Conflict Management

Vistelar's training focuses on addressing the entire spectrum of human conflict at the point of impact from before an interaction begins through to the consequences of how an interaction is managed.

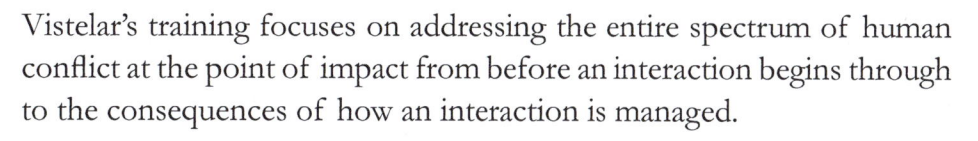

"Point of impact" is the short period of time when disagreements, insults or gateway behaviors, like swearing or aggressive posturing, can escalate to conflict and on to emotional and/or physical violence. Effective point-of-impact conflict management using Vistelar's methodologies ensures the best possible outcome for interactions with others and sets the stage for positive future interactions.

Vistelar's methodologies are not meant to address longer-term situations, such as ongoing relationship difficulties or lengthy negotiations. However, many of the principles and tactics you'll learn will have a positive impact on such situations.

Vistelar's 6 C's of Conflict Management: *Point-Of-Impact Conflict Management Framework*™ provides a means to analyze interactions and determine which conflict management tactic should be used in which phase of an interaction.

The blue boxes in the graphic below describe the three elements of all interactions:

- **Context**: Approach considerations prior to an interaction, such as assessment of risk and physical positioning, decision on whether to proceed and personal mindset.

- **Contact**: Interaction considerations, such as words used, tone of voice, facial expressions, eye contact, hand position, body language and posture.

- **Closure**: Follow-through considerations, such as ensuring the situation is stabilized, summarizing decisions, and reviewing the interaction.

The primary goals of these elements are non-escalation (conflict prevention), achieving the best possible outcome and establishing a positive foundation for any future interactions.

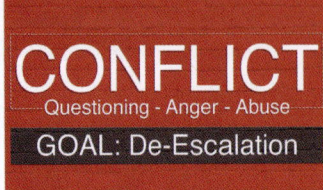

The red boxes in the graphic describe what can happen when interactions escalate:

- **Conflict**: When questioning, anger or verbal abuse enters into an interaction.
- **Crisis**: When the person with whom you are interacting is displaying at-risk behaviors.
- **Combat**: When resistance or aggression results in physical engagement initiated by either party.

The primary goals in the face of *Conflict*, *Crisis*, or *Combat* are de-escalation, everyone's safety, and shifting the situation to a positive outcome.

Note that all interactions have a *Context*, *Contact* and *Closure* element but only some interactions progress to *Conflict*, *Crisis* and/or *Combat*.

> *"Our job is to keep people on the blue brick road and off the red brick road."*
> Derrick S. Washington, Sr., retired Lieutenant, Milwaukee County Sheriff's Office

The "blue brick road" (the blue boxes) is where we want to keep an interaction. We certainly don't want to be the initiator of it moving to the "red brick road" (the red boxes). The only way an interaction should ever get on the "red brick road" is if others take us there. When that happens, getting back on the "blue brick road" should be the goal.

Chapter 5 :: Systemized Structure of Tactics

Systemized Structure of Tactics

Vistelar has created a *Systemized Structure Of Tactics*, outlined in this graphic, which makes our methodologies easy to learn, remember, apply and teach.

The remainder of this manual focuses on teaching the "how-tos" of each of the tactics listed.

Prior to getting started with this training, here is a brief orientation to this graphic.

Treat With Dignity By Showing Respect is listed first to highlight this core principle of customer service and conflict management.

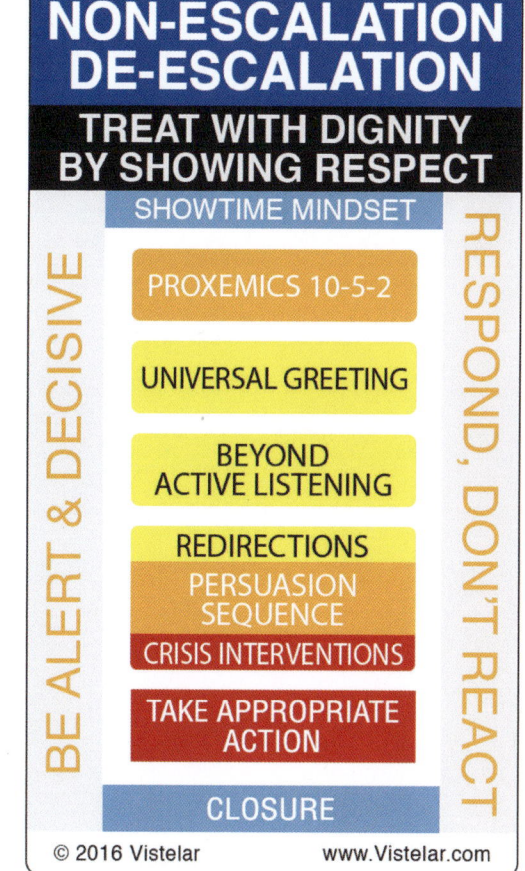

Be Alert & Decisive and *Respond, Don't React* are located on the sides to emphasize that these tactics should be considered at all times prior to and during an interaction.

Showtime Mindset is listed next to indicate that this tactic should be applied in advance of any interaction.

The above tactics as well as *Proxemics 10-5-2*, *Universal Greeting* and *Beyond Active Listening* are non-escalation tactics, with the goal of predicting and preventing conflict, and if necessary, turning a defensive atmosphere into a supportive one.

Redirections, *Persuasion Sequence* and *Crisis Interventions* are de-escalation tactics with the goal of recovering from a conflict or crisis situation.

Take Appropriate Action and *Closure* are ending-an-interaction tactics.

Closure is at the bottom of the graphic to indicate that this tactic should always be the final step of any interaction.

Here is a numerical listing of the eleven tactics:

1. Treat With Dignity By Showing Respect
2. Be Alert & Decisive; Respond, Don't React
3. Showtime Mindset
4. Proxemics 10-5-2
5. Universal Greeting
6. Beyond Active Listening
7. Redirections
8. Persuasion Sequence
9. Crisis Interventions
10. Take Appropriate Action
11. Closure

The graphic to the right provides a reminder of the details of some of these eleven tactics.

Chapter 6 :: Non-Escalation

Non-Escalation

Review and What's Next

So far you have learned the foundations of Vistelar's conflict management system:

- Conflict is inevitable
- Conflict can have positive or negative outcomes depending on how well it is managed
- Vistelar's *Core Principle, Five Approaches to Showing Respect, Empathy Triad* and *The Ultimate Goal*
- Importance of not speaking reactively

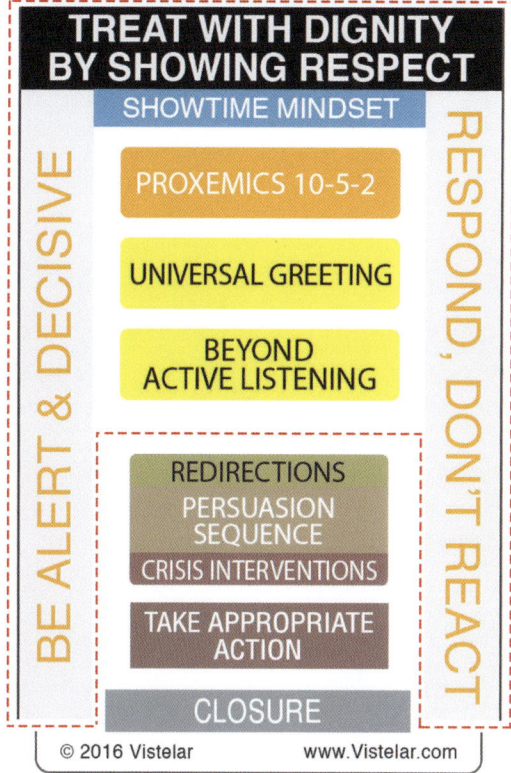

You have also learned about *Conflict Triggers*: yours, how to maintain your *Emotional Equilibrium* and how to not set off the triggers of others.

Finally, you have been introduced to Vistelar's *Point-Of-Impact Conflict Management Framework™* and *Systemized Structure of Tactics*.

Next, non-escalation tactics will be discussed — tactics focused on predicting and preventing conflict and, if necessary, turning a defensive atmosphere into a supportive one. These tactics include:

- *Treat With Dignity By Showing Respect*

- *Be Alert & Decisive; Respond, Don't React*
- *Showtime Mindset*
- *Proxemics 10-5-2*
- *Universal Greeting*
- *Beyond Active Listening*

In addition, practicing these tactics will improve your relationships with customers, colleagues, friends and family and enhance your confidence to deal with conflict head-on, rather than shying away from it.

These tactics are used primarily during the *Context* and *Contact* elements of an interaction.

> *"Think how much time you could save if you spent more time on non-escalation versus working on de-escalation after the contact escalated"*
> Gary T. Klugiewicz, VDI Director of Training

Framework: Context and Contact

In this section, you will learn Vistelar's non-escalation tactics — those that apply to these two elements of Vistelar's 6 C's of Conflict Management: *Point-Of-Impact Conflict Management Framework*™.

Context: Approach considerations prior to an interaction, such as assessment of risk and physical positioning, decision on whether to proceed, and personal mindset.

   Goal: prepare for the interaction

Contact: Interaction considerations, such as words used, tone of voice, facial expressions, eye contact, hand position, body language and posture.

   Primary Goal: non-escalation to prevent conflict and begin on a positive note

   Secondary Goal: turn a defensive atmosphere into a supportive one

As you progress through this section, consider how the non-escalation tactics you are learning apply to these first two elements of an interaction.

1. Treat With Dignity By Showing Respect

Treat People With Dignity By Showing Respect is the core principle of customer service and conflict management and serves as the foundation of everything Vistelar teaches.

Treating people with dignity is an acknowledgement of everyone's intrinsic value as human beings and showing respect is how you treat people with dignity.

Here is a review of how to show people respect:

1. See world through their eyes
2. Listen with all senses
3. Ask and explain why
4. Offer options, let them choose
5. Give opportunity to reconsider

Empathy is the engine that drives the effectiveness of all Vistelar customer service and conflict management tactics, which is accomplished by applying the *Empathy Triad*:

- Acknowledge their perspective
- Seek to understand
- Anticipate their needs

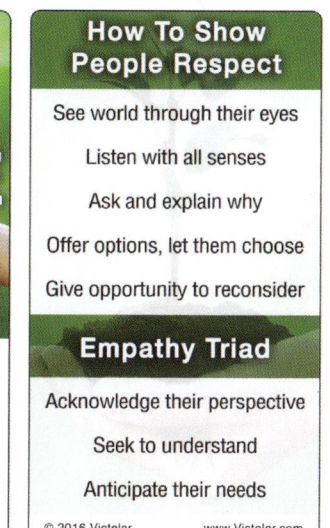

2. Be Alert & Decisive | Respond, Don't React

At all times when out in the world but especially when on patrol, pay attention to your surroundings and be ready to take action if you sense a safety risk, either from emotional or physical violence (*Be Alert & Decisive*). Then, when verbal or physical action is necessary, thoughtfully respond rather than impulsively react (*Respond, Don't React*).

As explained in the original *Street Survival Seminar:* 1) if you are not paying attention, you will never see the assault coming. The great equalizer in life is getting hit with a baseball bat from the blind side; 2) if you are not decisive and willing to make a decision, you have given control of the situation to the other person; and 3) if you have not planned and practiced your response, your response is a fantasy that could rapidly turn into a tragedy. If you haven't practiced your plan, you do not know if it will work in real world applications.

> "Warning: proper response requires that you: 1) remain alert; 2) be decisive; 3) have a preplanned, practiced response in mind."
> Gary T. Klugiewicz, VDI Director of Training

Implicit Bias

The *Respond, Don't React* tactic keeps you safe but there is also evidence it can prevent people from acting on their implicit biases.

Even well-meaning people frequently harbor hidden prejudices[7]. Studies have shown these subtle biases are widespread and associated with discrimination in legal, economic, and organizational settings.

Recent research[8] suggests that people have the capacity to override their worst instincts — if they are able to reflect on their decision-making as opposed to acting on their first impulse.

> *"When people made their decisions swiftly — in a few seconds or less — they were biased in their punishment decisions. Not only did they punish out-group members more harshly, they also treated members of their own group more leniently. But we also found that people could overcome these biased instincts if they engaged in rational deliberation. When people had the chance to reflect on their decision, they were largely unbiased, handing out equal punishments to in-group and out-group members."*
>
> Daniel A. Yudkin and Jay Van Bavel
> The Roots of Implicit Bias, *The New York Times*, Dec. 9, 2016

Here is how to *Be Alert & Decisive*:

- Constantly scan your environment with as many senses as you can. You should be listening and visually scanning several seconds ahead of where you are going, and try not to be distracted by phones or other technology. The more distracted you are within your environment, the more vulnerable you are to it.

> *"You can observe a lot by just watching."*
> Yogi Berra, American professional baseball player and coach (1925 - 2015)

Being aware of a verbal or physical threat, even seconds in advance, may keep you safe by giving you time to act instead of react.

- Do not ignore behaviors that give you feelings of uneasiness. If you feel unsafe, be decisive and either do not enter, or if appropriate for the situation, leave. Trust your intuition.

> *"Never discredit your gut instinct. You're not paranoid. Your body can pick up on bad vibrations. If something deep inside of you says something is not right about a person or situation, trust it."*
> Spirit Science

GATEWAYS TO VIOLENCE
- ANTISOCIAL ACTIONS
- VEILED THREATS
- OVERT THREATS
- VIOLENCE

Chapter 6 :: Non-Escalation

- Practice "when-then thinking" (a concept developed by Vistelar advisor, Coach Bob Lindsey) — plan what you will do "when" a verbal or physical incident happens, rather than thinking "if this happens, then I will ..."

  You should have a preplanned, practice response to situations where conflict could occur and decide in advance your plan of action should things escalate. Your plan should include verbal tactics, escape routes, how to get help, and physical alternatives.

- Consider level of risk (e.g., presence of weapons) and be aware of threat indicators, signals that your safety may be compromised because the communication with another person is breaking down. The most important indicators to watch for are the other person's:

  - Inability to manage distance, which is a reflection of your and the other person's safety and comfort level

  - Failure to control position, which is an indicator of the other person's respect or disrespect towards you

  - Tone of voice / word choice / excessive repetition, which is an indicator of the other person's frustration and anger

  - Hand movement, which is an indicator of the other person's ability to take action

  - Eye focus, which is an indicator of the other person's intent

- Be aware of gateway behaviors, which are antisocial actions that might not make you feel threatened at the moment, but have been shown to be reliable predictors of violence. Examples include: yelling, cursing, name-calling, verbal disrespect, aggressive posturing and veiled threats. Note this possible progression: antisocial actions ➔ veiled threats ➔ overt threats ➔ violence.

- Assigning a color code (originated by Jeff Cooper, internationally known firearms instructor) to situations can be helpful in assuming the appropriate level of caution.

Other than within the safety of your own home, never assign a color below yellow; you should not ever be totally oblivious to what is going on around you.

- Practice this tactic, so beyond just having the knowledge as to what to do, you also have the skills and abilities to *Be Alert & Decisive — Respond, Don't React* in the face of both verbal and physical threats and incidents.

Ethical Intervention

Be Alert & Decisive, *Respond, Don't React* apply to when you see a partner or colleague taking an action he or she will likely regret or that will get him or her in trouble.

In such circumstances, you have an obligation to step in, "tap out" your partner or colleague (verbally or physically) and take over the interaction — to execute an Ethical Intervention. As a contact professional, your job is to keep everyone safe: verbally if you can, physically if you must.

If you ignore their actions, you are condoning them.

"Officers should be obligated to intervene when they believe another officer is about to use excessive or unnecessary force, or when they witness colleagues using excessive or unnecessary force, or engaging in other misconduct."

PERF: 30 Guiding Principles On Use Of Force — March 2016

When faced with such situations, all of the *Be Alert & Decisive* and *Respond, Don't React* strategies apply: situational awareness, being attentive to gateway behaviors and threat indicators, when-then thinking, assigning a color code, and thoughtfully responding rather than impulsively reacting.

3. Showtime Mindset

In advance of any interaction where you anticipate or are faced with conflict, whether in person or on the phone, establish a *Showtime Mindset*. Imagine yourself stepping onto a stage to give a performance.

- Clear your mind of whatever else might be going on in your life, put aside any negative feelings or prejudices
- Focus all your attention on your audience
- Get all elements of communication — words, tone of voice and non-verbals — in alignment with the situation.
- Act as if other people are your equal, no matter who they are

Here are the specific steps to establish a *Showtime Mindset*:

1. Say to yourself, "It's *Showtime*!"
2. Stack your blocks; adopt an assertive posture
3. Take a deep breath through your nose, pause, and blow the breath out through your mouth
4. Put on the appropriate facial expression for the situation
5. Use positive self-talk — say to yourself, "I've got this."
6. Step onto the stage

Note: with the prevalence of video cameras, every interaction is likely being recorded. Therefore, from

Chapter 6 :: Non-Escalation

the moment you leave home, stepping onto a stage does not need to be imagined — it is actually real. It really is *"Showtime."*

> ### Please Note ...
>
> In very stressful situations, the third step in the *Showtime Mindset* sequence can be accentuated with autogenic breathing — a technique used to minimize the effects of the body's "fight or flight" mechanism. Here are the steps:
> - Breath in for a count of 3
> - Hold breath for a count of 3
> - Exhale for a count of 3
> - Repeat as needed — paying attention to your inhaling and exhaling — until your *Emotional Equilibrium* is under control

Effective use of the *Showtime Mindset* tactic requires all elements of communication to be in alignment with the situation. Just like an actor on stage, your words, tone of voice, facial expressions, eye contact, hand position, body language, posture and physical positioning must all send the same message.

> *"Since you never get a second chance to make a first impression, remember to control your body language and facial expressions."*
> Dave Young, Arma Director of Training

In addition, it is important to realize, in the midst of conflict, your non-verbals are often the most important element of your message. For example:

- You cannot overcome non-verbals that express lack of confidence, such as avoiding eye contact, slouching and looking anxious, with confident-sounding words and tone of voice.
- You cannot overcome threatening non-verbals, like staring, toe-to-toe positioning and aggressive posturing, with calm-sounding words and tone of voice.

Using the right words and tone of voice are important, but your non-verbals are often the primary driver of the outcome. That is why establishing a *Showtime Mindset* is an essential starting point for all interactions where you anticipate or are faced with conflict, with citizens, within your agency and in your personal life.

> *"Much of 'spoken' communication is actually non-verbal in nature. Facial expressions and gestures, and vocal elements such as 'tone of voice' can be equally important to the words that are said. In many situations, the listener trusts and believes the non-verbal cues more than the actual words. Understanding these non-verbal elements can make police officers more effective in communicating, which can help to de-escalate volatile situations."*

PERF: Integrating Communications, Assessment, and Tactics Training Guide For Diffusing Critical Incidents — October 2016

Relative to step #4 — "Put on the appropriate facial expression for the situation" — you need dozens of faces to draw upon (not just one stock face) so you can select the best one to harmonize with the goal at hand: e.g., pleasant, sad, calm, stern.

Please Note …

While *Showtime Mindset* is primarily a face-to-face interaction tactic, it also has application when communicating by telephone. While people cannot "see" the results of steps #2 and #4 (assertive posture, appropriate facial expression), they can certainly "feel" the results.

Do not think for a moment that, when on the telephone, your non-verbals do not come across loud and clear.

Another way to think about *Showtime Mindset* is to consider what math symbol is floating over your head when you begin interacting with another person, a technique originated by Vistelar advisor Master Chan Lee. Our non-verbals communicate messages to other people long before we ever open our mouths. In any given interaction, in relationship to the other person, ask yourself: Do you look less-than (< : passive), greater-than (> : aggressive) or equal-to (= : assertive)?

To be effective at conflict management, the equal-to (= : assertive) symbol is what you are after. You do not want to look passive or aggressive to the other person; you want to appear as his or her confident equal.

Sounding, projecting and responding with confidence, as if you are the other person's equal, gives you the best chance of starting an interaction on a positive note.

To drive home this point in our youth anti-bullying programs, we get the kids on their feet and have them yell out these lines in unison.

- You are how you sound!
- You are what you project!
- You are how you respond!

What we have found is that kids are not bullied due to some personal characteristic, like weight, race or sexual orientation. Instead, it is because others perceive them as vulnerable, as having a less-than (<) symbol floating over their head. Sometimes, just teaching a bullied child to project a *Showtime Mindset* is enough to cause the bullying to stop.

Just like the kids in our anti-bullying programs, your goal should be to appear as the confident equal of the person with whom you are interacting. You might try repeating the phrases above to yourself to get accustomed to having a *Showtime Mindset*.

Chapter 6 :: Non-Escalation

> ### Your Team Is Watching
>
> If you are a supervisor, realize your team members are watching you carefully and all the time. They are constantly trying to figure out which employees you favor or do not favor, which ideas you support or are against, which team behaviors you value, and the nature of your *Conflict Triggers*. They are paying attention to every little thing you do: what you say, your tone of voice and non-verbals — everything. So, when interacting with your team, remember it is always *Showtime*!

4. Proxemics 10-5-2

Proxemics is the study of the human use of space. Your physical presence — distance, relative positioning and hand placement — affect the comfort level of people interacting with you and your personal safety, whether you are dealing with citizens, colleagues, friends or family members.

This tactic is obviously extremely important for law enforcement professionals.

To be effective with proxemics:

- Be respectful of other people's personal space: the area which, if encroached upon, causes most individuals to feel discomfort, anxiety or anger. This distance varies by culture, but generally is two to four feet. Do not get too close without asking permission.

- When approaching people, introduce yourself from an appropriate distance and ask permission before coming closer (see *10-5-2* below).

- Stand at an angle to another person rather than directly in front of him or her. This position is less threatening and enables you to more easily escape if there is a safety concern.

- Maintain distance and positioning that prevents another person from ever being able to attack you from behind. The best way to never have someone grab your hair or put you in a rear chokehold is to never put yourself in a position where such an attack is possible. For example, when guiding a person to another location, always follow the person with your hands up rather than allowing him or her to follow you.

- When in close proximity to someone, keep your hand placement above your waist with open palms. This is a signal of honesty, indicates you are not hiding something and is a better hand position from which to block a physical attack.

PROXEMICS 10-5-2

- DISTANCE

- RELATIVE POSITIONING

- HAND PLACEMENT

Relative to the distance element of proxemics, there are three points where you should evaluate the risk level before moving closer, whether you are approaching a person or he or she is approaching you.

Relative to the distance element of proxemics, there are three points where you should evaluate the risk level before moving closer, whether you are approaching a person or he or she is approaching you.

- 10 Feet: Evaluation / Exit — At this distance, if you do not feel safe or are not prepared to become involved, you are far enough away to completely avoid the situation. Alternatively, you can deliberately decide to move closer.

- 5 Feet: Communication / Evade — At this distance, if the situation still seems safe, you are close enough to begin a verbal interaction, with an emphasis on listening with all your senses. Alternatively, you can flee.

- 2 Feet: Operation / Escape — At this distance, you are actively operating in the situation, but if things go badly, you must be prepared to escape.

In our live classes, we teach and practice a series of proxemic tactics that represent the application of the above principles. Below are pictured some of these tactics.

One-hand stop sign	Two-hand stop sign	Emergency timeout
Thinker stance	Guiding hands	Tactical sitting

5. Universal Greeting

When you first interact with someone — especially if you are a person of authority — these four questions generally pop into people's heads:

1. Who are you?
2. What gives you your authority?
3. Why are you interacting with me?
4. What's in it for me?

If you do not immediately answer these questions, the other person will often:

- Feel inhibited from communicating with you
- Fill in the blanks with incorrect answers, such as misidentification as to who you are; assumption you believe he or she is doing something wrong; or expectation the interaction is going to take a long time
- Feel disrespected

Any of these outcomes could cause an interaction to start on a negative note or even escalate. The *Universal Greeting* tactic prevents these outcomes. It has four steps:

1. **Appropriate greeting**
2. **Name and affiliation**
3. **Reason for contact**
4. **Relevant question**

Here is an example:

> "Good morning.
> I'm Officer Jones with the Springfield Police Department.
> The reason I approached you is because you look lost.
> May I help you?"

For the delivery, just like with *Showtime Mindset*, make sure all elements of communication — words, tone of voice, and non-verbals — are in alignment with the situation. Speak calmly and in a moderate volume. Do not respond to a raised voice by raising your own voice. Put on the appropriate facial expression for the situation. Adopt a non-threatening posture and hand position.

The *Universal Greeting* explains who you are, your source of authority and the reason for your contact, and then encourages the other person to talk. This a) establishes a positive initial contact, b) develops rapport and c) is the ultimate in showing respect. Then, through listening with all your senses to his or her answer to your relevant question, it gives you an opportunity to learn more about this person: active intelligence gathering.

If you already know the other person, still use this greeting but add his or her name to Step #1 and skip step #2 ("Good morning Bob. The reason I …").

You should move deliberately through the four steps to not delay giving the other person a chance to talk. Only then, should you deal with other matters, such as providing further explanation, giving an estimate of expected duration, asking for identification or answering his or her additional questions.

The *Universal Greeting* is called this for a reason: it is universal. You should use it to begin almost any encounter: with citizens, within your agency and in your personal life.

Here are some additional examples:

Professional

"Good evening.
I'm Officer Jones with Springfield Police.
The reason I'm here is because we received a call about loud music.
Would it be possible to lower the volume?"

"Good afternoon.
I'm Officer Jones and this is Officer Smith with Springfield Police.
The reason we stopped by is because we received a call reporting a suspicious person walking through the area looking into car windows.
Have you seen anyone doing this?"

UNIVERSAL GREETING
- APPROPRIATE GREETING
- NAME AND AFFILIATION
- REASON FOR CONTACT
- RELEVANT QUESTION

Within Your Agency

"Good Afternoon.
My name is Tony Martinez and I'm an officer in District 6.
The reason I'm calling is that I'm dealing with some personal issues at home and will need to take a couple of days off next week.
Can we please schedule a meeting to discuss?"

"Good morning Mr. Edwards
This is Officer Jackson from the 3rd District
The reason I've called is to schedule my car for a service inspection because the "check engine" light is lighting up.
Can we schedule something today?"

Chapter 6 :: Non-Escalation

In Your Personal Life

"Good Afternoon.
My name is Sue Carpenter and I am the mother of Evan who is in your 5th grade class.
The reason I'm calling is because I am concerned Evan is being picked on in class.
Do you have a few minutes to talk about how we can keep Evan safe at school?"

"Good Afternoon Officer.
My name is Dave Johnson and I'm Dr. Carlin's patient.
The reason I'm calling is my tooth is hurting and I would like to schedule an emergency appointment.
Can you get me in to see Dr. Carlin today?"

"Good Afternoon.
My name is Angie Lee and I'm a police officer in town.
This is my first time at this event.
How are you folks doing?"

Please Note ...

The *Universal Greeting* is just as applicable in written communications as in verbal. When writing a letter or email, always start with the four steps: an appropriate greeting, your name and affiliation, the reason for your contact and a relevant question.

An email could start with something as simple as this:

"Good Afternoon. It is Officer John Smith with District 5. The reason I'm writing is to ask for a couple of days off to attend an upcoming wedding. Can I take October 22 and 23 as vacation days?"

Always start your written communications with the *Universal Greeting* and they will be much more effective.

Start every professional and personal interaction with the *Universal Greeting* and you will increase the likelihood of beginning on a positive note and not escalate a situation unnecessarily.

> *"The reason to deliver a great Universal Greeting is to create a reasonable doubt in your contact's mind that you are not a jerk."*
>
> Gary T. Klugiewicz, VDI Director of Training

Perspective Taking - Interlude

Empathy can be difficult. In our live training, we often show a video of a college-classroom situation where the end point is a woman being taken to the ground and handcuffed. Then, we ask half the students to take the perspective of the individuals of authority (college teacher and law enforcement professionals) and the other half to take the perspective of the woman (student in class). Next, we ask each side to share their assigned perspective with the whole class.

As you can imagine, it is often difficult for those whose profession is teaching or law enforcement (individuals of authority) to take the perspective of the woman — and for non-law-enforcement individuals in class to take the perspective of the individuals of authority. In fact, it is quite difficult.

You have already learned the Core Principle of Vistelar's conflict management methodology (treat people with dignity by showing respect) and the Empathy Triad (acknowledge their perspective, seek to understand, anticipate their needs), which should always be applied to your interactions with people, even if you disagree with them.

As a law enforcement professional, there are times when you need to extend these principles further and apply them even if you do not respect the other person's behavior.

You might view a person as a hardened criminal but, to be effective at conflict management and have the best chance for a positive outcome, you must treat him or her with dignity and work hard to take his or her perspective.

As stated earlier, dignity is an inalienable right of all human beings so your opinion of other's behavior should have no effect on your ability to take their perspective (practice Empathy) and treat them with dignity.

6a. Listening Introduction

Empathy is a professional approach for communicating concern and gathering information about another person: active intelligent gathering. It is the engine that drives the effectiveness of all Vistelar customer service and conflict management tactics.

The *Universal Greeting* begins this process, and following the relevant-question step, it continues with the *Beyond Active Listening* tactic.

Whether you are interacting with a citizen, colleague, friend or family member, your level of *Empathy* for the other person will determine your success.

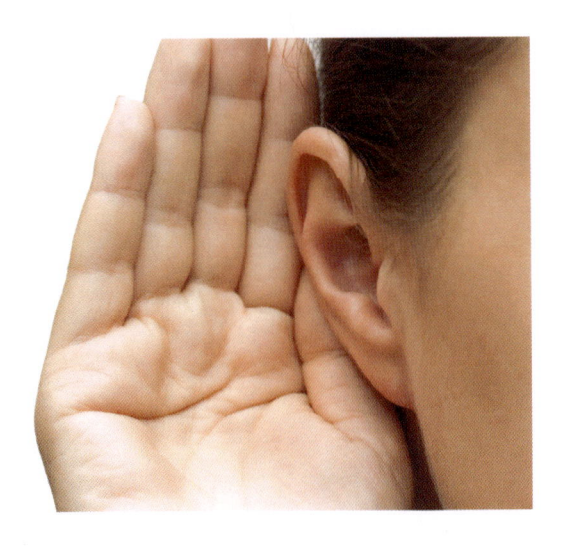

Empathy is a challenge when you first meet a person because you know little about him or her, which makes taking that person's perspective difficult. However, you can still apply the first element of the *Empathy Triad*: acknowledge their perspective. Whatever the other person might say, you can respond with statements like: "Thank you for sharing that with me." — "Hmm, I never thought of it that way." — "Huh, that's interesting."

Chapter 6 :: Non-Escalation

Once you have gathered additional information about the other person, you can apply the second two elements of the *Empathy Triad*:

1. Seek to understand the other person. Try to understand his or her perspective so you can treat the individual the way you would want to be treated if you were that person and in the exact same circumstances. The better you can understand the other person's perspective, the more effective you will be with customer service and conflict management.

2. Anticipate the other person's needs. Consider what that person will be thinking or feeling immediately following the interaction, the next day or later. The goal is to treat the other person the way that person may not even know he or she wants to be treated.

The *Beyond Active Listening* tactic begins with applying the following *Active Listening* techniques.

- Focus all your attention on the other person. Do not check your watch, phone or the clock.
- Keep arms and legs uncrossed. Do not fidget.
- Put on the appropriate facial expression for the situation
- Maintain appropriate eye contact
- Nod, and if appropriate, take notes to acknowledge points made
- Make brief comments like: "Tell me what is going on" — "Talk to me a bit" — "Go On" — "Really?" — "I see" — "Tell me more" — "And then what happened?"
- Listen with all your senses. Besides just hearing the other person's words and tone of voice, be attentive to visual cues like facial expression, eye contact, posture, and body language; how he or she smells, been drinking?; via touch, the person's level of tenseness; and even how the air might taste, smoker?
- Let the other person finish a complete thought before responding

The goal of *Active Listening* is for the other person to feel: a) he or she has been heard and understood, and b) you are interested in what he or she is trying to communicate.

> *"One of the most sincere forms of respect is actually listening to what another has to say."*
> Bryant H. McGill, author, Nobel Prize nominee (1969 to present)

To be effective at customer service and conflict management, you should listen more than you talk; that is why we have two ears and one mouth. When other people are talking, you should be listening.

What usually happens instead? When the other person is talking, you are probably thinking about what you are going to say next. Far too often, people are so busy formulating a response they do not hear a word of what the other person is saying.

> *"Listen with the intent to understand, not the intent to reply."*
> Stephen Covey, *The 7 Habits of Highly Effective People* (1932 - 2012)

Listen to understand and learn. Your brain will have plenty of time to figure out what to say next after the other person has finished talking.

6b. Beyond Active Listening

The *Beyond Active Listening* tactic enables you to gather more information about a person (active intelligence gathering) than what you might learn through just *Active Listening*, with the goal of increasing your effectiveness at customer service and conflict management.

You must realize that people frequently do not say what they mean, especially in conflict situations. Their words are often smoke screens to mask what they are really thinking and feeling. That is why *Active Listening* is rarely sufficient. You must dig deeper by going *Beyond Active Listening*.

> *"If you are only listening with your ears, you are not hearing everything"*
>
> Dave Young, Arma Director of Training

If you do, you will be amazed what you can learn about the needs, wants and desires of another person, which you can then use to be more effective at preventing and managing conflict and delivering exceptional customer service.

There are six elements of the *Beyond Active Listening* tactic:

1. **Clarify** — Ask questions with the goal of learning more about the other person; however, so you don't come across as an interrogator, ask permission ("I've got some questions to ask – is that OK?" or "May I ask some clarifying questions so I better understand?") and ask open-ended and opinion-seeking questions.

2. **Paraphrase** — If you feel the need to interject yourself into the conversation in order to gain a better understanding about what a person is saying, start with "Let me see if I understand what you are saying." Then, repeat in your words what you believe is the meaning behind the other person's words – and ask if you are correct.

> *"Let me see if I understand what you are saying. "You are saying [and then share your interpretation of his or her words]. Do I have this right?"*

In addition to the "You are saying …" phrase, you can use other phrases, such as: "You are thinking …" — "It is your point of view …" — "It seems to you … " — "In your experience …" — "As you see it …"

This element helps you gather additional information about the other person and reduces the likelihood of misunderstandings. Be sure to always end this tactic with a confirming question.

Chapter 6 :: Non-Escalation

Note: if the other person is expressing strong emotions, it is often helpful to start with the *Reflect* element (see below) to acknowledge his or her feelings before using the *Paraphrase* element to express your understanding of the content of what the person is saying.

3. **Reflect** — Acknowledge the person's emotions and give him or her the opportunity to talk out his or her feelings (rather than act them out). After using your *Active Listening* skills, state your view of what the other person is feeling and why — succinctly and precisely as possible.

    "Hmmm. You're feeling anxious because you're not sure where your mom is. Do I have this right?"

    Keep your *Reflection* tentative and be sure to give the other person time to respond to your question.

    Note that strong emotions — anger, hate, fear — usually don't need reflecting because the other person is often well aware of these feelings. Instead, use the *Reflect* element to bring out more subtle emotions that the other person might not recognize he or she is feeling.

    This element helps you understand the nature and intensity of the other person's emotions. Be sure to always end this tactic with a confirming question.

4. **Mirror** — Subtly imitate the other person's subconscious body orientation, posture, mannerisms, breathing rate, eye contact, tone of voice and talking pace, but never his or her negative body language.

    This element can cause the person being mirrored to feel more connected with the person exhibiting the mirrored behavior. Therefore, it helps build rapport, trust and liking so the other person is more open to communicating with you. In addition, doing this can help you gain a better understanding of the person you are mirroring.

    Note: *mirroring* is different than *modeling calmness* (demonstrating the behavior you want the other person to replicate), which is covered in the *Crisis Interventions* section later in this manual.

5. **Advocate** — Acknowledge the issue and express how you and the other person should work together to address it. "That sounds like a big problem; let's work together to figure out how to fix it." or "That's unacceptable; let's both see what we can do about it."

    This element communicates concern and it gets the interaction correctly focused on the problem, rather than on you.

BEYOND ACTIVE LISTENING
- CLARIFY
- PARAPHRASE
- REFLECT
- MIRROR
- ADVOCATE
- SUMMARIZE

6. **Summarize** — At the end of an interaction, provide a detailed summary of what was decided and/or what will happen next, followed by a question asking for confirmation; e.g., "Let me see if we both understand what we agreed to" [and then share summary]. "Is that your understanding?"

This element ensures you and the other person are on the same page.

Even if you struggle to put yourself in another person's shoes because you have not had his or her life experiences, using the *Beyond Active Listening* tactic can help you comprehend the person's mental and emotional response to a situation, and in turn, increase your effectiveness at conflict management and providing exceptional customer service.

"When people talk, listen completely. Most people never listen."
Ernest Hemingway, American Novelist (1899 - 1961)

Remember the primary goals of the *Beyond Active Listening* tactic:

1. For the other person to feel he or she has been heard and understood

2. For the other person to feel you are interested in what he or she is trying to communicate

3. To gather information about the other person, which will help you in managing whatever conflict that might arise, such as his or her:

    - Intentions
    - Level of confidence
    - Ability to understand
    - Mental and emotional state
    - Mental health history
    - Medications he/she is taking or should be taking
    - Capabilities to deliver on a threat

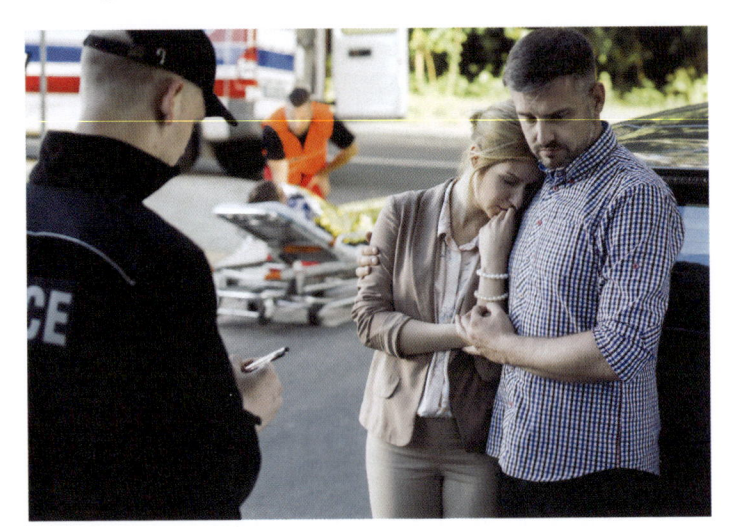

Chapter 6 :: Non-Escalation

People Are Listening To You

The people with whom you interact are also "listening" to you — and not just to your spoken words. Your tone of voice and non-verbals are equally, if not more, important to how people interpret your communications.

For example, in the paraphrase tactic, the words must be presented with neutrality (via a calm tone of voice and non-verbals). If not, the paraphrase will sound more like judgment than *Empathy* and will not be effective.

In addition, realize that periods of silence are a component of your communication, which you should not be afraid to use. Silence gives people an opportunity to collect their thoughts and removes pressure for their immediate response.

"The sounds of silence can never be misquoted."
Coach Bob Lindsey, Vistelar Advisor

Finally, when you are with others in addressing a conflict situation, have one person do all the talking to minimize confusion. Then, if this person is not able to engage the individual, switch roles.

Remember, people will generally not remember what you said. What will stick in their head is how you made them feel.

"The level of intensity of a person's attack is driven by how poorly you've made them feel."
Dave Young, Arma Director of Training

Chapter 7 :: De-Escalation

De-Escalation

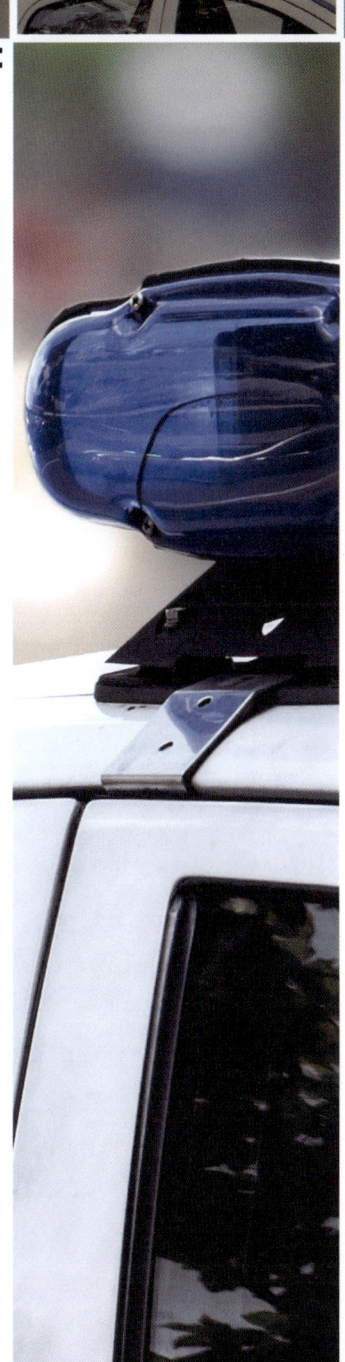

Review and What's Next

Up until this point, non-escalation tactics have been discussed. These tactics focus on predicting and preventing conflict, and if necessary, turning a defensive atmosphere into a supportive one.

- *Treat With Dignity By Showing Respect*
- *Be Alert & Decisive; Respond, Don't React*
- *Showtime Mindset*
- *Proxemics 10-5-2*
- *Universal Greeting*
- *Beyond Active Listening*

In addition, practicing these tactics will improve your relationships with citizens, colleagues, friends and family. And, if you struggle with conflict with any of these people and, as a result, avoid it or accommodate them by giving in, the use of these tactics will enhance your confidence to deal with conflict head-on, rather than shying away from it.

Next, de-escalation tactics will be discussed. These tactics focus on recovering from a conflict or crisis situation:

- *Redirections*
- *Persuasion Sequence*
- *Crisis Interventions*

The *Redirections* tactic is used when someone questions you, expresses frustration or anger, verbally abuses you, or is on a rambling tangent from what you are trying to accomplish.

The *Persuasion Sequence* is used when someone is questioning, resisting or refusing a request.

Crisis Interventions are used when someone is in crisis and displaying at-risk behaviors.

If a situation with another person has escalated to conflict or crisis, before using these de-escalation tactics, do your best to apply what you have already learned:

- Show them respect
- Take their perspective (*Empathy*)
- Don't speak reactively
- Maintain your *Emotional Equilibrium*
- Think "when then," not "if then"
- Imagine stepping onto a stage (*Showtime Mindset*)
- Respect their personal space
- Do not stand directly in front of them
- Control distance (*10-5-2*)
- Have a pre-planned escape route
- Answer their four questions (*Universal Greeting*)
- Give them an opportunity to talk and then listen with all your senses
- Acknowledge their perspective
- Communicate concern and gather information (*Beyond Active Listening*)

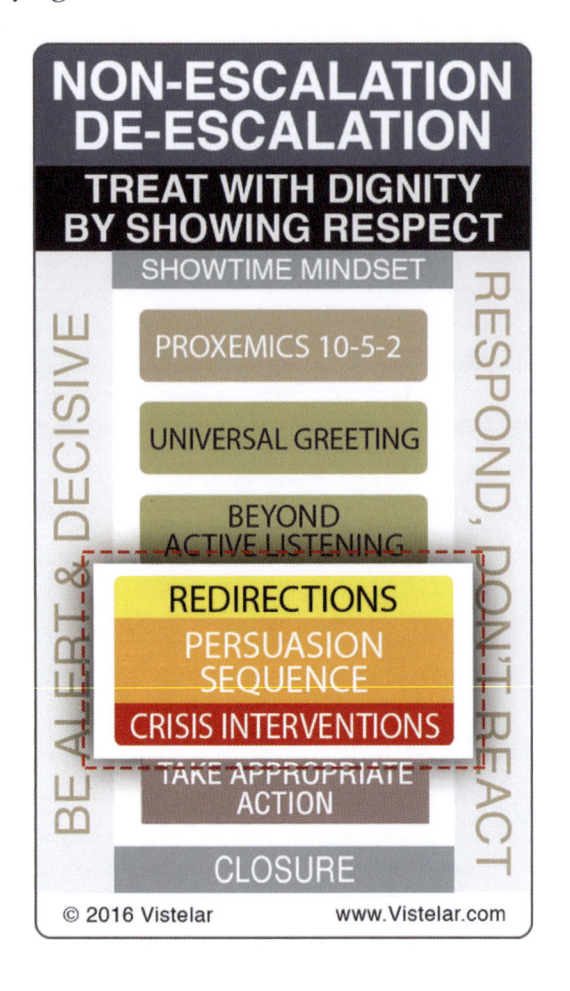

Notes:

- In most cases, prior to using any of the three de-escalation tactics (*Redirections, Persuasion Sequence, Crisis Interventions*), you should introduce yourself with the *Universal Greeting* and then listen to the other person's response to your "relevant question" using the *Beyond Active Listening* tactic.

- Although *Beyond Active Listening* is primarily a non-escalation tactic, it is useful in de-escalation. Encouraging another person to talk and then listening to him or her is the ultimate in showing of respect, so it can have a dramatic effect in calming a situation.

- The primary goals of the three de-escalation tactics (*Redirections, Persuasion Sequence, Crisis Interventions*) are everyone's safety and shifting the situation to a positive outcome.

- If you struggle in dealing with conflict, having the knowledge, skills and abilities to apply these three de-escalation tactics will significantly increase your confidence in addressing anger, verbal abuse, at-risk behavior and other clashes.

Framework: Conflict and Crisis

In this section you will learn Vistelar's de-escalation tactics that apply to these two elements of Vistelar's 6 C's of Conflict Management: *Point-Of-Impact Conflict Management Framework*™.

Chapter 7 :: De-Escalation

Conflict: When questioning, anger or verbal abuse enters into an interaction.

    Goal: de-escalation to prevent heightened emotions from progressing to crisis or a physical altercation.

Crisis: When the person with whom you are interacting is displaying at-risk behaviors.

    Primary Goal: everyone's safety.

    Secondary Goal: recovery, to end the crisis.

Note that all interactions have a Context and Contact element but only some interactions progress to Conflict and/or Crisis.

As you progress through this section, consider how the de-escalation tactics you are learning apply to these two elements of an interaction.

7. Redirections

The *Redirections* tactic is used when someone questions you, expresses frustration or anger, verbally abuses you, or is on a rambling tangent from what you are trying to accomplish.

Think about what you would do if someone threw a punch at you. Would you just sit there and take the punch? Obviously not. You would try to block or deflect it. You should do the same with a verbal punch — redirect it rather than just take it, or worse, get sucked in and end up in an argument or a fight.

Here is how the *Redirections* tactic works.

When someone verbally attacks you, respond with something like, "I hear you, but… ," and then either return to what you were trying to accomplish or leave, if leaving is appropriate for the situation.

Note the attack is acknowledged, but is not addressed. The goal of the *Redirections* tactic is not to accomplish the objective of the interaction; it is just to move past the attack and either get back on point or leave.

There are two types of *Redirections*:

    1. *Acknowledge* ➜ *Back To Issue*

    2. *Divert Attention*

With the *Acknowledge* ➜ *Back To Issue* type, there are two parts: 1) acknowledging his or her comments with a statement like "I appreciate that," "I hear you," "I got that," "I see," and 2) getting back to the issue at hand. Your message to the other person is that:

- You have heard them
- Their attack has no impact on you
- The interaction must be focused on your agenda, not theirs

REDIRECTIONS
- ACKNOWLEDGE ➜ BACK TO ISSUE
- DIVERT ATTENTION

Here are some examples of the *Acknowledge* ➜ *Back To Issue* type:

- "I hear you, however we have an issue to address; can you work with me here?"
- "I see and I'd probably feel the same way if I were in your shoes; nevertheless, you were driving twenty-five mile per hour over the speed limit and I have a job to do here."
- "I appreciate that. Other folks in the area felt the same way until they saw the facts. Let's review what we have here."
- "Whoa! Time out! Is there anything I can do to help? If not, can we get back to the issue?"
- "You might be right, but we still need to find a way to solve this problem."
- "I appreciate that you feel that way and I want to solve the problem. Can you work with me here?"
- "I get that you're upset. However, there are children present that don't need to hear that language. If you must use profanity, let's go outside while we figure this out."
- "I appreciate that you've had problems here in the past, but you haven't dealt with me before, so let's see what I can do to help."
- "You seem upset and I'm sorry you feel that way; however, can we get back to the issue at hand?"
- [If the other person is walking towards you with their hands up] "I appreciate that you're looking out for both our safety, but please put your hands down and let me know how I can help you."

The *Beyond Active Listening* elements of *Reflect* and *Paraphrase* can also be used as *Acknowledge* ➜ *Back To Issue* type *Redirections*. For example:

- "You're feeling frustrated because it took us a long time to get here; but, we're here now so let's see if we can figure out some way to resolve this."
- "Let me see if I understand what you are saying. What you are telling me is [and then repeat in your words what you believe is the meaning behind their words]. Do I have this right?"

These two tactics are respectful and effective ways to interrupt a verbal attack. By stating what another person is feeling or saying, he or she will almost always stop talking to listen to what you have to say. Then, you can take back control of the interaction.

Sometimes, even when you have adequately explained the reason for a situation, the other person will continue to ask "Why" over and over again and a Redirection can be effective. For example:

- "Sir, I've answered your question and explained why. Can we get back on track with why I'm here?"

When acknowledging the other person's comments, be careful not to say that you "know" or "understand" the other person's situation. Such statements could prompt an angry, "You don't know how I feel! — how could you?" type of response. Instead, start the *Redirection* with statements like: "I appreciate that," "I hear you," "I got that," "I see."

Also, be careful about using humor because it can sound disrespectful. *Redirections* should not sound like a counterpunch.

Becoming Bully-Proof

In our youth anti-bullying programs, the *Redirections* tactic is one of the main tactics we teach.

The bully yells, "You are an idiot" — and the practiced response is "I hear what you said -- was there something important you need to tell me?" and the child walks away.

Redirections are like a suit of armor that make kids (and adults) bully-proof.

The *Divert Attention* type of *Redirection* has the goal of giving the other person time to calm down or to forget why he or she is upset. In addition, it gives you the opportunity to leave if you sense a safety issue and if leaving is appropriate for the situation.

Here are some examples of this type:

- "Whoops, I think I see someone coming. Oh, false alarm — OK, where were we?"
- "What was that noise?"
- "I forgot my [keys, cell phone or needed form]. Give me a few moments."
- "The *Universal Greeting* — sometimes this approach to initiating a contact is so different than what people are used to, it can stop disruptive behavior in its tracks
- "I need to take a bathroom break. I'll be right back."

We had a client who made balloon animals. He would often interrupt a rant by saying, "By the way, what type of animal would you like to be?" Then, he would pull a balloon out of his pocket and make that animal. Once he had the animal made, he would get back to the business at hand.

When using the *Redirections* tactic, be careful to preserve the other person's dignity. This tactic is not a dismissal. No matter how badly you are being treated, you are still dealing with a human being and you need to treat him or her as such. Therefore, always question if the *Redirections* tactic is appropriate or if it would be better to listen to the other person in order to gather more information using the *Beyond Active Listening* tactic.

When dealing with verbal attacks, do not take the bait, defend your ego or lash out. Instead, focus on accomplishing your goal for the interaction, or if necessary and appropriate, leave the situation.

Do not concern yourself with the other person's abusive comments. Your job is not to fix his or her attitude; it is to get back on track with the goal of the interaction.

Note: the above scripted examples of *Redirections* are provided just to get you started in developing your own scripts you can put to memory and practice with colleagues, friends and family. When faced with real-world verbal attacks, just winging it does not work. Instead, you need lots of "arrows" in your quiver that you have memorized and are comfortable and competent in using, because you have engrained them into your mental muscle memory.

Therefore, please take the time to consider the situations you commonly face, write out appropriate *Redirections* scripts and practice those scripts out loud, ensuring the appropriate words, tone of voice and non-verbals are in alignment with the situation.

> *"If you don't tell them what to say you shouldn't be shocked on what comes out of their mouths."*
> Dave Young, Arma Director of Training

Once you become proficient at the *Redirections* tactic, you might start enjoying verbal attacks for two reasons:
- You know the other person cannot get under your skin and disrupt your *Emotional Equilibrium*.
- You are confident you have the knowledge, skills and abilities to respond, in an effective manner, to whatever the other person may throw at you.

Chapter 7 :: De-Escalation

> ### Ethical Intervention
>
> The *Redirections* tactic can be used to "tap out" your partner or colleague (*Ethical Intervention*) when you see them taking an action they will likely regret or that will get them in trouble. Just by stepping in you "acknowledge" the situation and then you can get things back on track with an appropriate statement, such as:
>
> - "Jim, let me ask a few questions here while you check the backyard. OK?"
> - "Jim, the computer in our squad isn't working; can you check it out? I'll take over here."
> - "Jim, my phone died and I need to talk with Mike regarding this. Can you go outside and call him? I will be out in a minute."

Relative to addressing verbal attacks, there is one more important point: stick to your lines. Do not partake in any negative side conversations or "trash talk," such as offhand remarks or derogatory comments that might be heard by others or caught on camera and come back to haunt you.

8. Persuasion Sequence

The *Persuasion Sequence* is used when someone is questioning, resisting or refusing a request.

The goal of the *Persuasion Sequence* is to provide an opportunity in a respectful manner for the other person to cooperate with your request before you are faced with taking whatever further action is necessary.

"Persuasion is often more effectual than force."

Aesop, Ancient Greek story teller
(620 - 564 BCE)

This tactic is almost always used following a four-step Universal Greeting, such as with a person driving over the speed limit:

> "Good morning.
> I'm Officer Jones with Springfield Police Department
> The reason I stopped you is because my radar showed you were going 55 in a 35 mile per hour zone. Is there any reason why you were driving so fast?"

Once the driver answers, you might ask him or her to provide a driver's license and car registration. If he or she questions, resists or refuses your request, you would use the Persuasion Sequence to try to get cooperation. In using this tactic, you should only progress to the next step if the previous step did not gain cooperation.

Here are the three steps of this tactic:

1. Explain why, confirm understanding

To prevent people from imagining their own reasons as to why you are asking them to do something, which can become a roadblock for cooperation: a) provide a reason for your request (usually due to a law, policy, rule or prior agreement), b) give them a rationale for the reason, and c) confirm their understanding of the reason.

> "The reason for my request is that the law states that anyone operating a motor vehicle must surrender their driver's license to any law enforcement officer, when requested, to confirm they are legally able and licensed to operate the motor vehicle. Do you understand?"

Then end this step by asking again for their cooperation. If they again, question, resist or refuse your request, you would progress to step #2.

2. Offer options, let them choose — a) present positive option(s); b) present negative or less-positive option(s); c) emphasize the positive option(s).

PERSUASION SEQUENCE
- EXPLAIN WHY, CONFIRM UNDERSTANDING
- OFFER OPTIONS, LET THEM CHOOSE
- GIVE OPPORTUNITY TO RECONSIDER

Do this using this script:
"We have some good options here" — and then:

a. Present a vivid description of the positive option(s)
b. Present a vivid description of the negative or less-positive option(s)
c. Put a final emphasis on the positive

Here is a generic example:

> "We have some good options here. If you cooperate, we can [and then share a positive option]. However, if you refuse, we will [and then share a negative or less-positive option]. It's your choice but can you work with me here?"

Here is an example specific to law enforcement:

> "We have some good options here. If you cooperate, you'll get home tonight, be able to feed the dog, tuck the kids in bed and sleep in your own bed. However, if you refuse, I am required to arrest you, call your spouse and tow your vehicle – and then you'll spend tonight in jail in the same cell with a couple of people I arrested earlier tonight. By the time you get home it will cost you more than $800 in bail and towing fees. It's your choice but I'd rather you get home tonight. Can you work with me here?"

If you have effectively practiced *Empathy*, you should be able to see the world through the other person's eyes, and make the positive option sound quite good and the negative or less-positive option sound much less attractive. In describing the two options, be as specific as possible and paint a vivid picture.

Then make it clear the choice is theirs, not yours, which takes all the pressure off of you and puts it on them. It is their decision as to what will happen next and they are empowered to make that choice.

> *"You have options. I don't have any options. I have a duty to perform."*
> Gary T. Klugiewicz, VDI Director of Training

By offering options to a person who is questioning, resisting or refusing a request, you are providing him or her with the opportunity to save face while agreeing to cooperate.

Always end this step by asking again for their cooperation. If they again, question, resist or refuse your request, you would progress to step #3.

3. Give opportunity to reconsider

If this final step of the *Persuasion Sequence* is needed, you would a) ask them to reconsider, and b) express a hope that he or she would do so.

For example:

- "You seem like a reasonable person. Would you please reconsider?"
- "Is there anything I can say to help you change your mind?"
- "I know we both want the safest solution possible. Would you please reconsider your decision?"

And then follow with a statement like, "I would hope so."

If the other person has not cooperated after this third step, your options here will vary depending on the situation. What is important is that you know your options and have a preplanned response to the situations you will likely face (see *Take Appropriate Action*).

> **Please Note ...**
>
> Even though "ask and explain why" is one of the five approaches to showing respect, there are times, such as the existence of a safety issue with immediate compliance required, when you must tell someone to do something rather than ask them. In such situations, issue a short, direct command.

At any time during *Persuasion Sequence*, you may need to use other tactics, such as *Beyond Active Listening* to hear them out or *Redirections* to address verbal abuse, so you can get back on track before continuing with the sequence.

When using the *Persuasion Sequence*, it is important each step is used without excessive repetition. You do not want to get into a cycle of providing exhaustive explanations, offering numerous options or giving multiple opportunities to reconsider. Instead, just move deliberately through each step, with the goal of providing an opportunity for the other person to cooperate before you are faced with taking whatever further action is necessary.

Think about the number of times someone, whether it is a citizen, a colleague, a family member or a friend, questions, resists or refuses a request.

"Why do I need to do that?" — "I'm not getting out of my car" — "I'm not giving that back" — "I'm not leaving" — "I'm going to miss that deadline" — "I can't give your money back" — "I won't be coming in on the weekend" — "I don't want to do my homework" — "I'm not going to bed."

Not everyone deals with verbal attacks or crisis on a regular basis, but no one can escape the daily experience of having people question, resist or refuse requests. That is why the *Persuasion Sequence* is the most used of the three de-escalation tactics.

9. Crisis Interventions

Introduction

Crisis Interventions are used when someone is in crisis and displaying at-risk behaviors.

A crisis occurs when an individual has an experience that exceeds his or her coping skills, which can happen to anyone. However, there are issues that can contribute to the frequency and severity of crisis, which can be classified as:

1. Long-term issues, such as psychiatric disorder, cognitive disability, addiction, or history of trauma
2. Under the influence issues, such as being actively affected by alcohol or drugs
3. Short-term issues, such as violence, sexual assault, relationship loss (death, divorce, abandonment), incarceration or financial loss.

Crisis often leads to a range of at-risk behaviors that can cause emotional or physical harm to the individual in crisis or to others. Therefore, it is important you know how to identify the various states of crisis and how to respond correctly to a crisis situation.

Generally, people in crisis do not act out because of the issues identified above (long term, under the influence, short term). Instead, their behaviors are due to over-stimulation, an urgent need, or both. These behaviors present along a continuum of states that can be classified as baseline, stress, acute and recovery.

- Baseline: behaviors typical for an individual's:
    - Natural Personality — shy, grumpy, outgoing, happy
    - Background — cultural upbringing, social development, history of trauma
    - Mental Health — cognitive disabilities, psychiatric disorders
    - Physical Health — chronic pain, diabetes, heart disease
- Stress: heightened anxiety, with these possible responses:
    - Physical: tremors, headache, rapid breathing, increased perspiration, fatigue

- Emotional: anger, panic, irritability, hopelessness, inappropriate emotions
- Behavioral: fidgeting, pacing, clenched fist, boxer stance, crowding, resisting
- Verbal: yelling, name calling, cursing, mumbling, blaming, interrupting, ignoring
- Nonverbal: inappropriate expressions, staring, target glancing, refusing eye contact
- Atypical: body rocking, hand flapping, shutting down, lashing out, repeating,

- Acute: unbearable anxiety, with these possible responses:
  - Loss of cognitive, emotional and/or behavioral control
  - Urgent need to end the emotional pain or stop the real or perceived threat
  - Direct threats to harm themselves or others
  - Physical violence against themselves or others

  Note: individuals with cognitive disabilities often stay in the acute state of crisis for long periods of time.

- Recovery: continued anxiety, but in process of returning to pre-crisis level of functioning with these possible behavioral responses:
  - Emotional: embarrassment, regret, rationalizing, apologetic
  - Behavioral: crying, calm, withdrawn, unresponsive, in denial, tired

  Note: individuals in the recovery state of crisis are at risk of returning to acute state.

Trauma Informed Care

If you are required to get involved in a crisis situation, it is important to understand the principles of Trauma Informed Care (TIC).

TIC is an approach to interacting with others that acknowledges the effects of psychological, emotional and physical trauma on people's behavior and considers these effects in how interactions are handled. TIC asks "What happened to you?" rather than "What is wrong with you."

Trauma can be classified as:

- Acute trauma: A single event — experienced or witnessed — of grave physical or emotional threat or harm, such as serious accident or illness, homicide, suicide, physical or sexual assault, military trauma, terrorism, natural disaster, or abrupt separation from a loved one through death, abandonment, incarceration, or other circumstance.
- Complex trauma: Prolonged exposure to traumatic experiences, such as neglect, maltreatment, domestic violence, substance abuse, mental illness, chronic illness, bullying, homelessness, poverty or war.
- Historical trauma: Cumulative wounding transmitted across generations within an ethnic or racial minority.
- Sanctuary trauma: Overt or covert traumatic experiences within mental health, educational, foster care, religious and other institutions.
- Secondary trauma: Learning about another person's trauma.

A history of trauma can lead to a vulnerability for re-traumatization — an action or situation that is a reminder of a traumatic event. Such a reminder can rapidly push a person from his or her baseline behavior state to a stress or even acute state of a crisis.

A "trauma informed" approach to interactions acknowledges this reality and emphasizes:

- The use of active intelligence gathering about an individual's trauma history in order to minimize the possibility of re-traumatization. Active intelligence gathering can be accomplished by debriefing with others who know the person, using the Beyond Active Listening tactic, and reviewing the person's medical history if available.

- The need to avoid reminding the individual of a traumatic event by not:
    - Blaming, shaming or labeling
    - Asking about the individual's trauma or forcing him or her to talk about it
    - Yelling or becoming angry when the individual acts out
    - Touching without permission and direction from a mental health professional, unless required by an emergency situation
    - Exposing the individual to people or situations that may serve as a reminder of the trauma event. Possible reminders include persons in uniform, superior or authoritarian attitudes, former tormentors or attackers, conversation, behavior, or media involving violence or sexual situations, and kissing or other public displays of affection by others.

Initial Goal: Everyone's Safety

The initial goal is any crisis situation is everyone's safety until the situation is stabilized, so make that your focus. Realize that the acute stage of crisis can happen quickly, with a response of physical violence.

When faced with an individual in crisis do not address the situation alone, unless there is no other option. Seek someone else to assist you, preferably a mental health professional. In addition, always be ready to call for backup.

Also, when approaching a person in crisis, be aware that some might be delusional, under the influence of drugs or alcohol, or have cognitive limitations due to dementia, Alzheimer's, a brain injury, or autism. Therefore, take these steps to keep everyone safe (originated by Jane Dresser, RN - Director, Medical-Psychiatric Nursing Consultants, Inc.):

1. Attempt to get their attention. Slowly move into their line of sight, ask politely for them to look at you, and slowly wave your hands.

2. Check their perception of reality — "Where are you?" — What time/day is it?" — "What are you hearing?" — "What do you see?"

3. Attempt to establish rapport and safety — "Mary, I'm here to help you" — "It's

Chapter 7 :: De-Escalation

okay, you're safe with me."

4. Explain your perception of reality — "Sam, you are in Johnson grocers" — "I can't hear what you are thinking" — "I don't see bugs, but come over here with me where it's safe" Note, you are not denying their reality; you are simply sharing yours.

5. Move towards resolution — "Alice, let's get you home. Who should I call?" — "Bill, tell me what you need right now, so I can help." — "OK, here is exactly what we are going to do …"

Promoting Recovery

Beyond safety, a secondary goal in a crisis situation is Recovery, a return of the individual to his or her pre-crisis level of functioning. The crisis intervention tactics presented below address this goal.

Many of the conflict management tactics presented earlier can assist with the goal of Recovery, such as:

- *Showtime Mindset*
- *Proxemics 10-5-2*
- *Universal Greeting*
- *Beyond Active Listening*
- *Redirections*
- *Persuasion Sequence*

These non-escalation and de-escalation tactics are invaluable during the baseline, stress, and recovery stages of crisis to prevent escalation to the acute stage. However, they may be less effective because they rely on rational thinking. Individuals in the acute stage of crisis typically lose cognitive and emotional control and may respond poorly, if at all, to questions, redirections or persuasion.

In these situations, there are additional strategies to use. As stated above, at-risk behaviors by an individual in crisis are generally due to over-stimulation, an urgent unmet need or both, which can be addressed via the use of these approaches (originated by Joel Lashley, Vistelar advisor and author of *Confidence In Conflict For Healthcare Professionals*).

1. **Reduce Stimulation:** less is better, as long as safety isn't compromised.

    - Manage proxemics: distance, relative positioning and hand placement — don't crowd, step back, stand at an angle, move slowly, keep hands in sight
    - Turn down the noise—soften your voice volume and tone; turn off/down televisions, radios, sirens, alarms, etc.
    - Soften the lights—turn them down if doing so doesn't compromise safety

2. **Separate and Support:** provide for the individual's privacy as much as possible.

CRISIS MANAGEMENT
- REDUCE STIMULATION
- SEPARATE AND SUPPORT
- ADAPT COMMUNICATION
- MEET URGENT UNMET NEEDS

- Take him or her to an area out of public view and, if that is not possible, dismiss onlookers. Keep enough trained staff on scene for safety, but out of site when feasible
- Provide support by calling in trained professionals, interpreters, and staff who have previously
- Model calmness by demonstrating the behavior you want the other person to replicate.
  - Practice reverse yelling—the quieter you get the quieter they will eventually get
  - Speak slowly if they are speaking fast
  - Breathe calmly and deeply if they are hyperventilating
  - Display the appropriate non-verbals – if you want them to be concerned, look concerned; if you want them to be unafraid, look confident

Note: all behavior equalizes – people will match your behavior if it is appropriate and consistent. Telling or asking people to calm down does not work, but you can lead them down by modeling the behavior you are seeking.

3. **Adapt Communication:**
   - Slow the interaction down
   - Use a "one voice" approach where only a single person talks to the individual. One voice = communication; two voices = noise; three or more voices = chaos
   - Wear the appropriate expression — show confidence, concern, empathy
   - Frequently use the individual's name to build an emotional connection and help the other person follow the conversation and stay engaged
   - Give only one direction or ask only one question at a time
   - Use five or less simple words per sentence to make it easier for the individual to process your comments
   - Pause frequently and offer up to 20 seconds of silence before repeating yourself, to ensure the individual has the needed time to process your comments
   - Make a safety statement like: "You're safe with me; let me help"
   - State the obvious, such as: "You were in a car accident"

4. **Meet Urgent Unmet Needs:**

   People in crisis cannot begin recovery if they have an urgent need that is not being addressed. Offering water, food, toileting, privacy, a blanket, a phone call, or whatever else a person in crisis might not be able to ask for on his or her own will often quickly normalize behaviors and is a showing of respect — one of the most important human needs.

Relative to touching a person in crisis, the general rule is that you should not do so, unless an emergency situation requires it to keep the individual or others safe.

Remember, the primary goal in a crisis situation is everyone's safety until the situation is stabilized. Recovery, a return of the individual to his or her pre-crisis level of functioning, should be considered a secondary goal.

Ethical Intervention

In the heat of the moment, your partner or colleague could lose the ability to cope with a situation. This would require you to execute an Ethical Intervention, which could be as simple as saying: "Knock it off," or "I'm going to write this up as I see it." Remember that, as a contact professional, your job is to keep everyone safe — verbally if you can, physically if you must.

Chapter 8 :: Ending an Interaction

Ending an Interaction

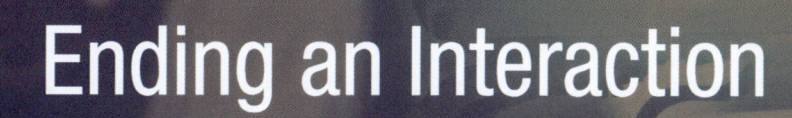

Review and What's Next

Up until this point, you have learned the following customer service and conflict management tactics:

- Non-escalation tactics, for predicting and preventing conflict, and if necessary, turning a defensive atmosphere into a supportive one.
    - *Treat People With Dignity By Showing Respect*
    - *Be Alert & Decisive; Respond, Don't React*
    - *Showtime Mindset*
    - *Proxemics 10-5-2*
    - *Universal Greeting*
    - *Beyond Active Listening*
- De-escalation tactics, focused on recovering from a conflict or crisis situation:
    - *Redirections*
    - *Persuasion Sequence*
    - *Crisis Interventions*

The primary goals of these three de-escalation tactics are everyone's safety, and shifting the situation to a positive outcome.

If you struggle in dealing with conflict, having the knowledge, skills and abilities to apply these three de-escalation tactics will significantly increase your confidence in addressing anger, verbal abuse, at-risk behavior and other clashes.

Next, tactics related to ending an interaction will be discussed:
- *Take Appropriate Action*
- *Closure*

The *Take Appropriate Action* tactic is used when the *Persuasion Sequence* has ended without cooperation or there is a clearly articulable safety concern.

The *Closure* tactic is used at the end of an interaction to achieve the best possible outcome and establish a strong foundation for the next interaction.

Framework: Combat and Closure

In this section you will learn Vistelar's ending-an-interaction tactics that apply to these two elements of Vistelar's 6 C's of Conflict Management: *Point-Of-Impact Conflict Management Framework™*.

Combat: When resistance or aggression results in physical engagement initiated by either party.

    Goal: physical safety

Closure: Follow-through considerations, such as ensuring situation is stabilized, summarizing decisions, and reviewing the interaction.

    Primary Goal: achieve best possible outcome

    Secondary Goal: establish positive foundation for any future interactions

Note that only a few interactions progress to Combat, but all interactions have a Closure element.

As you progress through this section, consider how the ending-an-interactions tactics you are learning apply to these two elements of an interaction.

10. Take Appropriate Action

Despite best efforts, non-escalation and de-escalation do not always work:

- *Persuasion Sequence* can end without cooperation or be clearly inappropriate.

    There can be many reasons this can occur. Even if you correctly used all the non-escalation/de-escalation tactics taught in this manual, other factors affecting people's behavior may have a stronger influence. For example, they may be intoxicated, mentally ill or undergoing a medication reaction. Or they may choose not to cooperate just because they do not like the consequences of cooperation.

- A clearly articulable safety concern can occur that justifies taking action based on the totality of the circumstances known to you at the time.

TAKE APPROPRIATE ACTION
- PERSUASION SEQUENCE ENDS WITHOUT COOPERATION
- CLEARLY ARTICULABLE SAFETY CONCERN

When either of these criterion is met, the *Take Appropriate Action* tactic should be used, which includes these two steps:

- Know your options for taking action
- Have a preplanned response to situations you will likely face ("when-then thinking")

Your options for *Taking Appropriate Action* will vary according to your role within your organization, the environment you are in, the established policies and procedures, defined rules of engagement and your training and experience.

Here are some possibilities that can be used alone or in combination:

- Monitoring the situation until help arrives
- Escorting or transporting the person to another location
- Control alternatives
    - Escort holds
    - Compliance holds
    - OC spray
    - Electronic control devices
    - Decentralization techniques
- Protective alternatives
    - Vertical stuns
    - Focused strikes
    - Incapacitating techniques
    - Intermediate weapons
- Deadly force

What is extremely important is that, in both your professional and personal lives, you have a planned response to what you will do when it is necessary to *Take Appropriate Action*.

> *"Although rules of engagement may differ, tactics remain constant at the same level of escalation based on application and environment."*
>
> Gary T. Klugiewicz, VDI Director of Training

Ethical Intervention - Interlude

Ethical Interventions were previously mentioned in this manual within the sections covering these tactics:
- Be Alert & Decisive, Respond, Don't React
- Redirection
- Crisis Interventions

Again, the goal of an *Ethical Intervention* is to prevent or stop an incident when you believe a partner or colleague is about to take an action that he or she will likely regret or that will him or her in trouble (e.g., setting off *Conflict Triggers* of others, acting out due to anger, excessive or unnecessary use of force).

This topic is being covered again here because it is an application of *Take Appropriate Action* – the tenth element on the Non-Escalation / De-Escalation graphic.

An *Ethical Intervention*: requires you remain alert, be decisive and have a preplanned, practiced response in mind. Early intervention is the key.

> *"Ethics are more values in action."*
>
> Jack Hoban, author of *The Ethical Protector – Police Ethics, Tactics and Techniques* and Subject Matter Expert for the U.S. Marine Corps.

Jack's point with this quote is that it is moral to know a situation is inappropriate, but it is ethical to take action on that knowledge.

The distinction between morals and ethics can be explained by Jack's playground example. Most people know that the bullying of a child is wrong (they have strong morals in respect to bullying). Less people are willing to take action to protect the bullied child (to demonstrate ethical behavior).

As law enforcement professionals, when we see inappropriate behavior we must be ethical (by doing an *Ethical Intervention*), not just moral. There are no innocent professional bystanders.

Your ability to intervene hinges on:
- Whether or not you feel a responsibility to act (your morals)
- Whether or not you feel you are capable of acting (your ethics)

There are three types of *Ethical Interventions*:

1. Pre-Incident Prevention — This begins with your *ethical presence* (what people expect of you based on your past behavior). Then the specific tactic is a verbal intervention implemented before the point of no return.

    Saying, for example, "It's Showtime — "knock it off" — "I'm going to write this up exactly how I see it."

Chapter 8 :: Ending an Interaction

Ethical Intervention - Interlude *continued*

2. Direct-Contact Override — stepping in to take over the interaction, using the appropriate level of override for the situation.

    - Level 1: Verbal — e.g., "Jim, let me ask a few questions here while you check out the backyard."

    - Level 2: Positioning — getting between your partner and the subject and, if necessary, moving your partner out of the way

    - Level 3: Physical — physically removing your partner from the scene

3. Delayed Post-Incident Remedies — if an incident occurs, doing the right thing following the incident (e.g., apologize where appropriate, debrief incident to improve future performance, notify supervisor, write up the incident).

    For example, being willing to write up an incident that went wrong.

As a contact professional, your job is to keep everyone safe: verbally if you can, physically if you must. If you ignore a partner's or colleague's inappropriate actions, you are condoning them.

Before reading on, take a few minutes to consider your own experiences with the inappropriate behavior of a partner or colleague. Were you ethical in your response or just moral? Do you have a social contract with your partner as to how each of you is expected to behave in such situations?

Here is what one of our students said to his partner to establish a social contract:

> *"I am the most loyal partner you will ever have. I've got your back. I do not owe you nor will I give you my career, my marriage or family, my house or, most certainly, my freedom. Don't ever put me in a position where I may have to risk those for you and I guaranty you I will never put you in a position where you may have to risk them for me."*
>
> Rob Shiller, Detective with Denver Colorado Police Department

Combat Is A Possibility

Combat — when resistance or aggression results in physical engagement initiated by either party — is always a possibility when dealing with conflict.

As stated earlier, Vistelar's training focuses on addressing the entire spectrum of human conflict at the point of impact — from before an interaction begins through to the consequences of how an interaction is managed. In other words, our training is a system of non-escalation and de-escalation coupled with physical alternatives.

Combat Is A Possibility *continued*

This manual is only focused on non-escalation and de-escalation. Our physical alternative training is provided via other courses, including;

- P.O.S.C.® 1 & 2 — Principles of Subject Control
- Non-Lethal Weapons
- Lethal Weapons
- Over 50 additional specialized courses

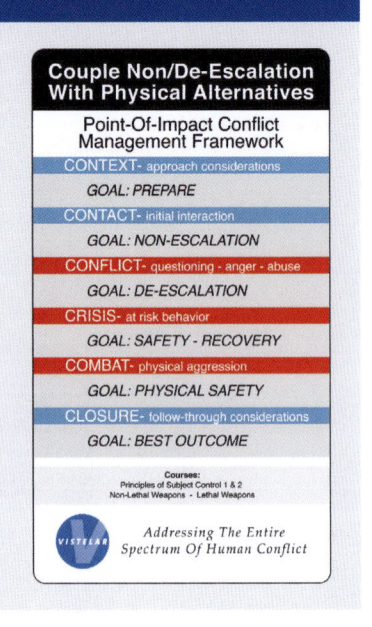

Couple Non/De-Escalation With Physical Alternatives

Point-Of-Impact Conflict Management Framework

| CONTEXT- approach considerations |
| GOAL: PREPARE |
| CONTACT- initial interaction |
| GOAL: NON-ESCALATION |
| CONFLICT- questioning - anger - abuse |
| GOAL: DE-ESCALATION |
| CRISIS- at risk behavior |
| GOAL: SAFETY - RECOVERY |
| COMBAT- physical aggression |
| GOAL: PHYSICAL SAFETY |
| CLOSURE- follow-through considerations |
| GOAL: BEST OUTCOME |

Courses:
Principles of Subject Control 1 & 2
Non-Lethal Weapons - Lethal Weapons

VISTELAR — *Addressing The Entire Spectrum Of Human Conflict*

11. Closure

The *Closure* element of Vistelar's *Point-Of-Impact Conflict Management Framework*™ (6 C's of Conflict Management) includes all follow-through considerations, such as ensuring the situation is stabilized, summarizing decisions, and reviewing the interaction. The two goals of *Closure* are to:

1. Achieve the best possible outcome; in a conflict situation, end the interaction in a better place than where it started

2. Establish a positive foundation for any future interactions
   To meet these goals, you should try to end all interactions with a positive *Closure*. Realize you can do everything well up to this point, and if the *Closure* step is handled incorrectly, a negative outcome can result.

> *"Remember the law of primacy and law of recency — because people usually remember the beginning and end of an incident while the middle gets muddled."*
> Gary T. Klugiewicz, VDI Director of Training

For a routine interaction, such as with a car stop with no conflict or crisis, *Closure* can be as simple as offering a genuine thank you. However, it is best to not use a scripted response or catchphrase, such as "Have a nice day" or "No problem," which can sometimes result in a citizen complaint.

Instead, treat people as individuals by providing a personalized *Closure* statement. Rather than treating people as another number, treat them as human beings.

If you have practiced *Empathy* (active intelligence gathering) during the interaction, you will have plenty to work with. Identify something unique to the other person on which to comment.

Chapter 8 :: Ending an Interaction

Note that not using a scripted response or catchphrase is even more important in situations with conflict or crisis.

At the end of more complex interactions – especially if there was conflict or crisis – follow these steps:

- If the interaction required use of de-escalation tactics or *Combat*, ensure the situation is stable (verbal attacks stopped; recovery from crisis, appropriate action taken; everyone is safe), an initial medical assessment is performed, and if appropriate, the necessary medical care is provided. More specifically:
    1. Check their emotional level
        - Give them affirmations that they are safe and will be OK
    2. Evaluate their levels of responsiveness and alertness
        - Carefully observe
        - Ask them questions like, "What is the day of the week?" - "What time is it?" - "What color are your shoes?"
    3. Verify any physical injuries
        - Blood, bruising, broken bones
        - Trouble breathing

- Use the *Summarize* element from *Beyond Active Listening*, where you review what was decided and ask for confirmation – "Let me see if we both understand what we agreed to" [and then share detailed summary]. "Is that your understanding?" Summarizing ensures everyone is on the same page and there are no misunderstandings.

- If an interaction has gone badly, set a positive foundation for any follow-on interaction by expressing your hope for a better next encounter and by not doing anything that would poison another contact, such as using sarcasm or parting shots.

- Here are some examples of possible Closure statements for various situations:

    At the end of a routine interaction:
    - "If you have no additional questions for me, please take your time while pulling back into traffic."

    At the end of an interaction involving conflict or crisis:
    - "I'm sorry we didn't meet under better circumstances, but I'm glad we were able to work through this matter. You have my contact information; please contact me with any additional questions."

    At the end of an interaction involving an accident:
    - To check feelings of security:

        "You are safe now — it's over; let us take care of you — we are here to help."
    - To check mental alertness:

        "What is your name? — do you know where you are? — do you know what day it is?"
    - To check for any physical injuries:

        "Do you hurt anywhere? — does it hurt when you breathe? — can you wiggle your fingers/toes?"

Following an interaction, you should reflect on the interaction, either on your own or with another person, with the sole goal of improving future performance. This can be done verbally or in writing, via an incident report or other such documentation.

If a group debriefing is needed, follow these steps during the discussion:

- Initial wellness check
- How is everyone?
- What went well?
- What was learned?

During the debriefing everyone should try to see the situation through the eyes of both parties in the interaction. If each participant practices *Empathy*, you will be amazed as to what the group will learn to improve future performance.

If the incident requires it, you should capture the debriefing on paper. A good written incident report, especially if your actions matched the training you received, is a powerful defense if anyone questions what happened in a specific incident.

"Remember, if you don't write it down and it would make you look good, it didn't happen."

Gary T. Klugiewicz, VDI Director of Training

Note: if you always follow the tactics taught in this manual, it will be much easier to write a complete and accurate incident report because you will know exactly what you did and the order you did it. You will also be much more equipped to justify your actions because you will be able to articulate exactly what you did (and said) when you were legally justified to do so.

Finally, take care of yourself. Effective conflict management is hard work, stressful and can wear you down. As a law enforcement professional, you are likely sensitive, caring and compassionate and probably chose your career to make a difference in some way. As a result, dealing with conflict, especially if it includes verbal and/or physical abuse, can be challenging.

Many of the tactics covered in this manual are meant to help with this challenge, such as:

- Treating people with dignity by showing respect, which does not mean you need to agree with the other person
- Practicing *Empathy* rather than sharing another person's distress (feeling sympathy)

GOALS OF CLOSURE
- ACHIEVE BEST POSSIBLE OUTCOME
- ESTABLISH POSITIVE FOUNDATION FOR FUTURE INTERACTIONS

- Knowing your conflict triggers and developing guards against them
- Scripting and practicing professional responses
- Having a *Showtime Mindset*
- Using *Proxemics 10-5-2* to enhance physical safety
- Knowing how to start any interaction (*Universal Greeting*)
- Using *Redirections* instead of just taking verbal abuse
- Offering options (*Persuasion Sequence*) to make it the other person's choice as to what will happen next, instead of yours
- Knowing how to respond to a crisis situation
- Having the confidence to take appropriate action if word-based tactics fail
- Using a post-incident debriefing process that is supportive instead of critical
- Knowing you can only control the process, not the outcomes

However, despite all this, you may still experience "burnout" or other emotional trauma. If that occurs, find someone to talk with or seek counseling.

The graphics displayed here are available from Vistelar as wallet-sized cards. These cards provide a helpful reminder of our tactics, but they can also be used:

- During a citizen complaint debriefing. You could pull out the "Non-Escalation De-Escalation" card (often nick-named the "get out of trouble" card) and walk through the card to explain exactly the steps you took during the interaction.

- If you are asked if you have had de-escalation training during a court testimony. You could pull out the "Treat People Right" card and walk through the two sides of the card (e.g., "Yes, I've learned to treat people right by treating them with dignity by showing respect. I also learned how to show people respect with these five approaches and how to practice empathy using the *Empathy Triad*.")

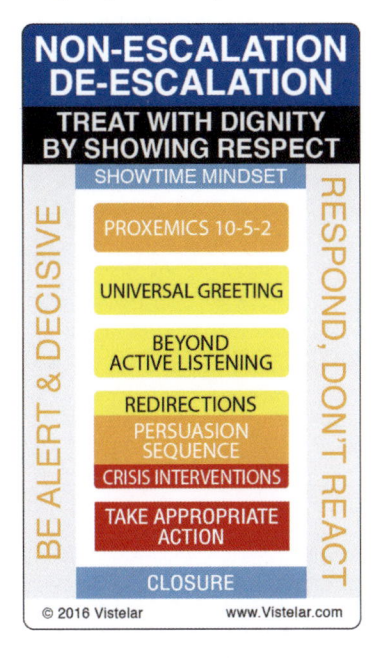

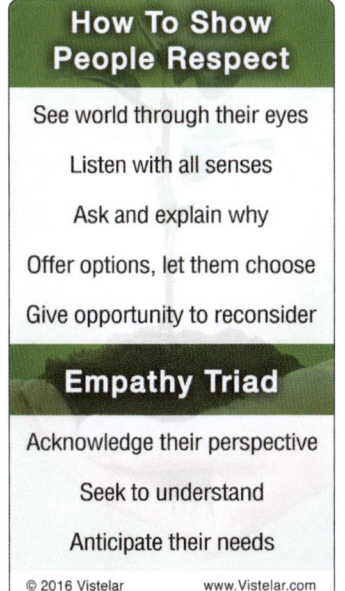

Chapter 9 :: Pulling It All Together

Pulling It All Together

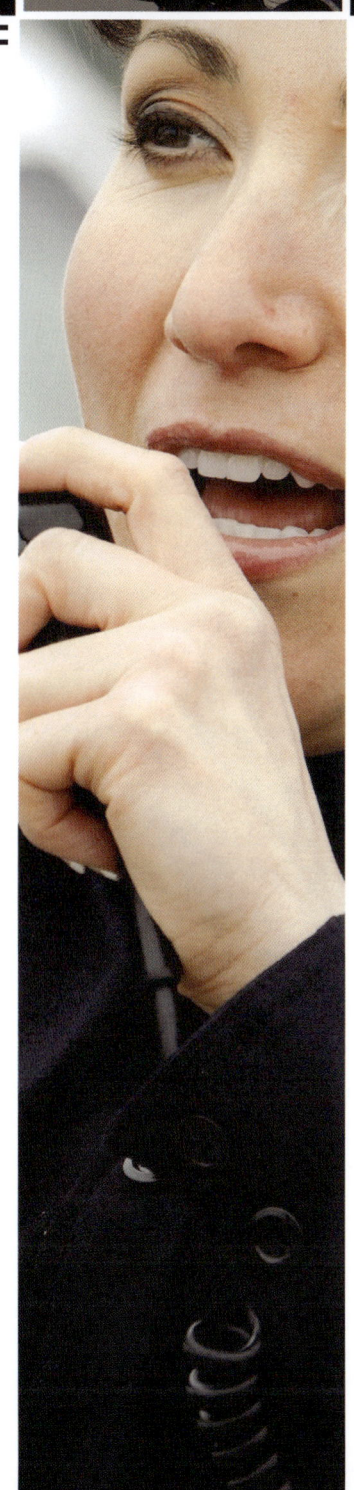

Review: Systemized Structure of Tactics

The emphasis throughout this manual has been on non-escalation, using the tactics of *Showing Respect*, *Practicing Empathy*, *Be Alert & Decisive*; *Respond Don't React*, *Showtime Mindset*, *Proxemics 10-5-2*, *Universal Greeting* and *Beyond Active Listening*.

When possible, it is always better to prevent conflict from starting, rather than having to use the de-escalation tactics of *Redirections*, *Persuasion Sequence* and *Crisis Interventions*.

- *Redirections*: when someone verbally abuses you, bullies you, or is on a rambling tangent from what you are trying to accomplish.

- *Persuasion Sequence*: when someone is questioning, resisting or refusing a request.

- *Crisis Interventions*: when someone is in crisis and displaying at-risk behaviors.

If used consistently, these de-escalation tactics enable you to decrease the intensity of conflict situations, maintain everyone's safety, and shift conflict situations to a positive *Closure*.

However, prior to using a de-escalation tactic, you should always ask yourself if it would be more appropriate to apply the tactic of *Beyond Active Listening* to see if there is any information you missed that could help in your management of the situation. Remember that you are dealing with a human being, so always be careful to preserve the other person's dignity.

At any point during an interaction, you should be ready to *Take Appropriate Action* if there is a clearly articulable safety concern. To do this, you must know your options and have a pre-planned response to situations you will likely face ("when-then thinking").

You should also be prepared to *Take Appropriate Action* if an individual continues to question, resist or refuse a request despite your efforts to give him or her every opportunity to cooperate by using the three-step *Persuasion Sequence*.

Finally, you should try to end every interaction with a positive *Closure* with the two goals of achieving the best possible outcome and establishing a positive foundation for any future interactions.

Beyond the above summary, here is a quick review of the principles and tactics you have learned in this manual.

- Treat people with dignity by showing respect
- Show people respect by:
  - Seeing the world through their eyes
  - Listening with all your senses
  - Asking and explaining why
  - Offering options and letting them choose
  - Giving an opportunity to reconsider
- Practice *Empathy* by applying the *Empathy Triad*:
  - Acknowledge the other person's perspective
  - Seek to understand the other person
  - Anticipate the other person's needs
- Don't speak reactively
- Know your conflict triggers and how to maintain your *Emotional Equilibrium* when faced with them
- Be careful your spoken words, tone of voice and non-verbals don't set off the *Conflict Triggers* of others
- Remain alert, be decisive and have a preplanned practice response in mind
- Establish a *Showtime Mindset* in advance of any interaction where you anticipate or are faced with conflict
- Be attentive to *Proxemics 10-5-2*
- Use the *Universal Greeting* in all initial interactions
- Actively listen, and when conflict arises, go *Beyond Active Listening*
- De-escalate conflict situations with:
  - *Redirections*

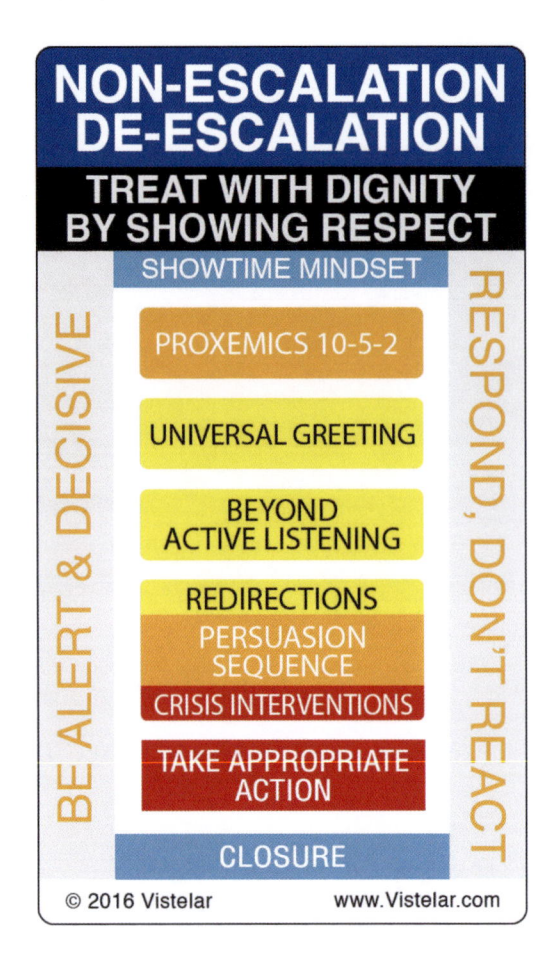

NON-ESCALATION DE-ESCALATION
TREAT WITH DIGNITY BY SHOWING RESPECT

BE ALERT & DECISIVE — RESPOND, DON'T REACT

- SHOWTIME MINDSET
- PROXEMICS 10-5-2
- UNIVERSAL GREETING
- BEYOND ACTIVE LISTENING
- REDIRECTIONS
- PERSUASION SEQUENCE
- CRISIS INTERVENTIONS
- TAKE APPROPRIATE ACTION
- CLOSURE

© 2016 Vistelar www.Vistelar.com

HOW TO SHOW PEOPLE RESPECT
See World Through Their Eyes
Listen With All Senses
Ask and Explain Why
Offer Options, Let Them Choose
Give Opportunity To Reconsider

UNIVERSAL GREETING
Appropriate Greeting
Name & Affiliation
Reason For Contact
Relevant Question

DE-ESCALATIONS
Empathize: Clarify - Paraphrase - Reflect
Mirror - Advocate - Summarize

Redirect: Acknowledge → Back To Issue

Persuade: 1) Explain Why 2) Offer Options
3) Give Opportunity To Reconsider

Crisis Management: Reduce Stimulation
Separate & Support - Adapt Communication
Meet Urgent Unmet Needs

Courses
Conflict Management For:
Gatekeeper Staff - Contact Professionals - Crisis First Responders

VISTELAR
Addressing The Entire Spectrum Of Human Conflict

- *Persuasion Sequence*
- *Crisis Interventions*
• Plan for when word-based tactics fail, and when necessary, *Take Appropriate Action*
• Effectively close every interaction

> ### Core Principle Revisited
>
> The core principle of customer service and conflict management that serves as the foundation of everything Vistelar teaches is:
>
> **Treat people with dignity by showing respect even if you disagree with them.**
>
> The primary reason to do this is because acknowledging people's inherent value as human beings, no matter what the circumstances, is the human thing to do.
>
> This quote emphasizes this point. We treat people right because of who we are, not in response to who they are or how they may be behaving.
>
> *"We treat people like ladies and gentlemen not necessarily because they are, but because we are."*
>
> North Dakota Highway Patrol

Framework: Six Cs Of Conflict Management

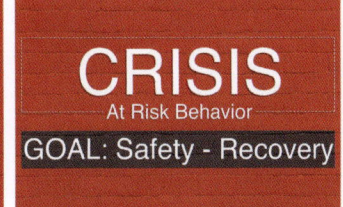

CONTEXT — Approach Considerations — GOAL: Prepare

CONTACT — Initial Interaction — GOAL: Non-Escalation

CONFLICT — Questioning - Anger - Abuse — GOAL: De-Escalation

CRISIS — At Risk Behavior — GOAL: Safety - Recovery

COMBAT — Physical Aggression — GOAL: Physical Safety

CLOSURE — Follow-Through Considerations — GOAL: Best Outcome

Let's return to how the non-escalation, de-escalation and ending-an-interaction tactics apply to Vistelar's *Point-Of-Impact Conflict Management Framework*™.

The blue boxes in the graphic describe the three elements of all interactions.

The primary goals of *Context*, *Contact* and *Closure* are non-escalation, achieving the best possible outcome, and establishing a positive foundation for any future interactions.

The red boxes in the graphic describe what can happen when interactions escalate.

The primary goals in the face of *Conflict*, *Crisis* or *Combat* are de-escalation, everyone's safety, and shifting the situation to a positive outcome.

Note that all interactions have a *Context*, *Contact* and *Closure* elements but only some interactions progress to *Conflict*, *Crisis* and/or *Combat*.

Please think back to the tactics you've learned and consider as to which element of an interaction each tactic would be most likely used.

Inconsistency Is The Enemy Of Peace

In many situations, an individual can interact with multiple police officers during a single encounter. If each officer treats this individual differently, especially if he or she is displaying bad or criminal behavior, it can be a recipe for disaster.

For example, this can happen in law enforcement where the first responders are managing the situation competently but then backup arrives and causes havoc.

In any environment where several people interact with a single individual, it is critically important that everyone consistently applies effective conflict management principles and tactics. Otherwise, the inconsistency in how a person is treated can actually make things worse.

> *"Inconsistency is the enemy of peace."*
> Joel Lashley, author of *Confidence In Conflict For Healthcare Professionals*

If you have one officer using the skills learned in this manual, but then have other officers "speaking reactively" and blurting out what first pops into their mind, the situation will likely escalate. You don't want one officer using the appropriate tactics, another ignoring the situation, someone else killing the individual with kindness, a fourth officer defending their ego to save face and someone else doing things that set off the individual's conflict triggers.

Such inconsistency will almost always empower a badly-behaving individual to escalate his or her actions.

In contrast, if an individual is acting out and everyone interacting with that person consistently applies the appropriate conflict management principles and tactics, the likelihood of a positive *Closure* is much greater.

BE CONSISTENT IN HOW YOU TREAT PEOPLE

INCONSISTENCY IS THE ENEMY OF PEACE

Another Strategy To Reduce Conflict

There is another conflict management strategy that is often ignored, but can have a significant impact on the prevalence of conflict within a law enforcement agency — both with the general public and employees.

This strategy is to fix operational issues. For example, with parking citations, if you limit payments to one station during normal business hours, you can prevent a great deal of conflict by allowing payment 24/7 at any district station.

Here are some other examples of operational fixes that can prevent conflict:
- Eliminating or automating steps in a process
- Streamlining bureaucratic procedures or decision processes
- Proactively notifying people of a problem rather than waiting to be contacted
- Reducing or simplifying paperwork

If you apply your new powers of *Empathy* to your operations (seeing the world through the general public's and your employees' eyes), you will be amazed at the ideas for friction-reducing fixes you come up with.

Fixing operational issues so the general public and your employees never have to deal with problems that could cause them conflict is, for a law enforcement agency, is one of the best ways to treat people with dignity.

Management Is Still Required

Effective conflict management at the point of impact — with citizens, at meetings, in one-on-one discussions, in the hallway, at lunch and within project teams — has immediate benefits.

In addition, it also lays the groundwork for longer-term positive outcomes, such as increased customer satisfaction, reducing citizen complaints, collaboration instead of compromise, people not avoiding conflict or accommodating it by giving in and improved team performance.

However, well-managed conflict is just part of the equation for long-term success. For example:

- If citizens and employees are treated with dignity, they will feel more emotionally safe and be more willing to share their concerns and problems, but someone still needs to address the concerns and fix the problems.
- Arguments among employees will be productive instead of destructive, but people still need to know how to collaborate and negotiate true win-win agreements.
- Conflict will get resolved rather than being allowed to fester, but management still needs to give clear direction, hold people accountable and evaluate performance.

Poorly-managed conflict at the point of impact is a huge roadblock to organizational performance, and addressing this issue can have a significant impact. However, it is not a cure-all — you still need strong management for all the benefits of effective conflict management to be realized.

SOCIAL CONTRACT

VOLUNTARY AGREEMENT BY ALL EMPLOYEES TO CONSISTENTLY TREAT EVERYONE WITH DIGNITY BY SHOWING RESPECT

And, relative to management, please remember *The Ultimate Goal* of the training provided by this manual — to develop a professional *Social Contract*: a voluntary agreement by all employees to consistently treat everyone with dignity by showing respect.

If you are a boss, start the "expectation contracting" process right way: make it crystal clear how you expect citizens and employees to be treated, set a good example and encourage members of your team to set an example — "I'm going to treat you with dignity by showing you respect. I ask the same from you".

A More Efficient Approach

We sometimes hear that, while Vistelar's conflict management tactics are extremely effective, they may not always seem the most efficient.

With citizens, it might seem more efficient to just tell them what to do, to not listen to them, and when asked why, to just say "because I told you so." And, with employees, it might seem more efficient to cut off debate, make a quick decision or ask people to hold their tongues.

However, that is false efficiency. The data[9] is crystal clear that using principles and tactics that show people respect just work better, so on the whole, they are far more efficient.

Sure, with citizens it takes time to really listen and not interrupt, to give explanations for your requests and to offer options from which to choose. And, with employees it takes time to not end a meeting until everyone has talked, to encourage people who are upset to express their frustrations, and to allow honest discussion without fear of retribution.

All this takes time, but in the short and long term, showing people respect is both more effective AND more efficient in managing conflict, delivering exceptional customer service and driving increased team performance.

Conflict Must Be Addressed Head-On

From the 1980s through the mid-2000s, Vistelar's trainers worked primarily with law enforcement who generally aren't shy about addressing conflict head-on.

Then, in the mid-2000s, we started working in other markets, such as healthcare, education and business where we found that many people struggled with conflict. As a result, they would avoid it at all costs or accommodate people by giving in just to appease them.

Conflict avoidance and accommodation can cause such problems as:

- Conflicts never getting resolved
- Resentment and lowered self-esteem
- Reinforcement of inappropriate behavior

- Conflicts actually escalating to emotional or physical violence

Vistelar's primary focus continues to be in working with "contact professionals," like police officers, who are comfortable with conflict but want to learn how to be more effective at managing it.

However, we find ourselves spending more and more time working with individuals and teams to provide them with the *knowledge*, *skills* and *abilities* to effectively manage conflict so they don't end up avoiding it or accommodating people by giving in. We want our students to be able to deal with conflict head-on, rather than shying away from it.

> *"In surveys of European and American executives, fully 85% of them acknowledge they have issues or concerns at work that they were afraid to raise. Afraid of the conflict that would provoke, afraid to get embroiled in arguments they did not know how to manage and they were bound to lose."*
>
> Margaret Heffernan, TED Talk: Dare To Disagree (1955 - present)

Just The Beginning

In managing conflict, there is a huge difference between knowledge, skills and abilities.

Knowledge — understanding a body of information related to the performance of a function

Skill — an observable competence to perform a learned psychomotor act

Ability — competence to perform an observable behavior in a real-world situation

DEVELOP THE ABILITY TO PERFORM YOUR CONFLICT MANAGEMENT SKILLS IN REAL-WORLD SITUATIONS

PRACTICE. PRACTICE. PRACTICE.

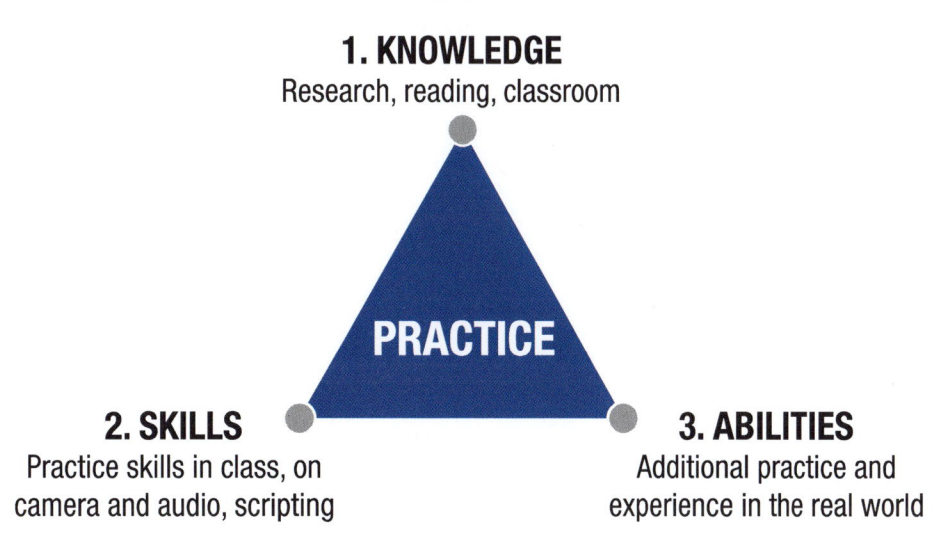

1. KNOWLEDGE
Research, reading, classroom

PRACTICE

2. SKILLS
Practice skills in class, on camera and audio, scripting

3. ABILITIES
Additional practice and experience in the real world

By reading and studying this manual, you can obtain the *knowledge* of how to be effective at conflict management. Vistelar's books, online courses and live workshops are other avenues for obtaining this knowledge.

However, when someone is dealing with conflict, just having *knowledge* is not nearly enough. You also need conflict-management *skills* including written scripts, and most importantly, the ability to perform those skills in real-world situations.

> *"Knowing is not enough; we must apply. Willing is not enough; we must do."*
> Johann Wolfgang von Goethe, German writer (1749 - 1832)

Therefore, please view this manual and other training you may receive from Vistelar as just the beginning. Please realize that, in real-world situations, managing conflict will rarely go as planned. Therefore, you must develop your conflict management *knowledge*, *skills* and *abilities* to a level where you can adapt to the situation and effectively handle whatever comes at you.

> *"Many skills – in particular, tactical communication skills – are perishable and need to be reinforced and practiced on a regular basis."*
> PERF: Integrating Communications, Assessment, and Tactics Training Guide For Diffusing Critical Incidents — October 2016

To move beyond from just having *knowledge* to having skills, you could attend an instructor-led online or in-person program where we provide the opportunity to demonstrate observable competence in the skills we teach.

Then, to develop your conflict management *abilities*, you could attend one of our longer classes where we have time for practice in simulations of real-world situations.

However, to become truly effective at conflict management, you must commit to further developing your *skills* and *abilities* by developing your own scripts for the situations you face, putting those scripts to memory, practicing those scripts using all three elements of communication (words, tone of voice, non-verbals) with friends, family members and colleagues, and using the principles and tactics you have learned in this manual in real-world situations.

> *"Training without practice is a fool's bet."*
> Dave Young, Arma Director of Training

When faced with real-world conflict, just winging it does not work. Instead, you need lots of "arrows" in your quiver that you have memorized and are comfortable and competent in using because you have baked them into your mental muscle memory via extensive practice and use.

Chapter 9 :: Pulling It All Together

Remember that effective conflict management is a performance so, before you go on stage, you must practice your lines, body language, facial expressions and stage positioning, as well as practice meshing the verbal elements of an interaction with the physical. Then, you need lots of stage time.

> *"Amateurs practice until they get it right. Professionals practice until they can't get it wrong."*
> Anonymous

Additional Information

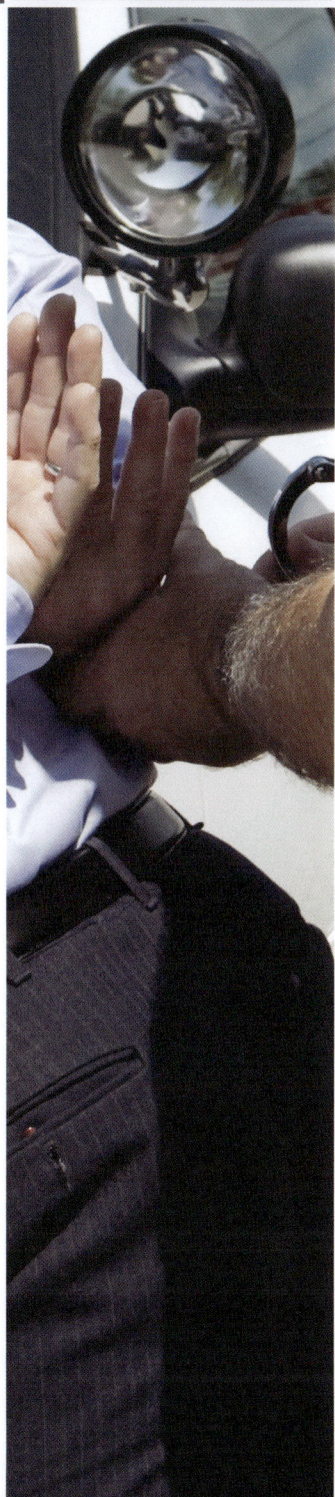

Fire Drills

All of Vistelar's in-person training programs use a "fire drill vs. fire talk" approach.

Class time emphasizes student interaction, scenario-based skill practice (using a proprietary video recording/review technology), analysis of real-life events captured on video, and memorable real-life stories ("peace stories") that illustrate the positive outcomes resulting from use of Vistelar's methodologies.

The goal of this approach is for our students to develop the knowledge, skills and abilities to manage real situations in the real world. However, there is never enough time in class to develop true proficiency.

Therefore, it is essential you practice the tactics listed below on an ongoing basis by developing "fire drills" optimized for your style of learning.

- *Conflict Triggers*
- *Treat With Dignity By Showing Respect*
- *Be Alert & Responsive; Respond, Don't React*
- *Showtime Mindset*
- *Proxemics 10-5-2*
- *Universal Greeting*
- *Beyond Active Listening*
- *Redirections*
- *Persuasion Sequence*
- *Crisis Interventions*
- *Take Appropriate Action*
- *Closure*

Other Resources

Vistelar offers our training via speaking engagements, workshops, and instructor schools using both live and online methods of instruction.

To download a description of Vistelar's law enforcement training programs, go to:

vistelar.com/course-descriptions

If you are a certified Vistelar instructor, you can access our Member Website by going to:

vistelaronline.com

Beyond the above, we obviously have much more to share about conflict management via our books, manuals, online programs, workshops, instructor schools and consulting services.

If you would like to learn more about what Vistelar offers, please access any or all of the additional resources listed below. We look forward to helping you further in better managing conflict in both your work and personal lives.

Live Training

Access our training calendar with registration information for upcoming in-person conflict management training programs —

www.vistelar.com/training-calendar

Get information about contracting with Vistelar to provide a customized conflict management training program for your agency, company, organization or group — www.vistelar.com/custom-onsite

Get information about hosting a Vistelar training program at your facility and receiving free slots in the hosted class — www.vistelar.com/host-a-class

Additional Information

Publications

Access our listing of online conflict management training programs, delivered using both virtual instructor-led and on-demand training methods — www.vistelar.com/online-courses

Access our online shopping cart with Vistelar books, manuals, online courses, workbooks, apparel and other products — www.vistelar.com/shopping-cart

Download a PDF of one or more of Vistelar's 16-page market-specific training program descriptions — www.vistelar.com/course-descriptions

Consulting

Get information about booking a Vistelar speaker to educate your

audience on such topics as conflict management, crisis intervention, personal safety awareness & protection, bystander mobilization, and workplace violence (including active shooter) — www.vistelar.com/speaking

Get information about Vistelar's workplace security/safety consulting services (review/analysis of and recommendations for: policies & procedures, environmental & procedural vulnerability, physical security technology, security personnel staffing, conflict management training) —

www.vistelar.com/consulting

About Vistelar

This manual was developed by Vistelar, a consulting and training institute focused on addressing the entire spectrum of human conflict at the point of impact — from before an interaction begins through to the consequences of how an interaction is managed.

Vistelar offers a wide range of training programs that address how to:

- Provide better customer service
- Predict, prevent and mitigate conflict
- Avert verbal and physical attacks
- De-escalate resistance, anger and abuse
- Control crisis and aggression
- Effectively manage physical violence

The results at the organizational level are:

- Higher levels of customer satisfaction
- Improved team performance, morale and safety
- Reduced complaints, liabilities and injuries
- Protected reputation, culture and business continuity
- Reduced harm from emotional and physical violence
- Decreased stress levels, lateral violence and bullying
- Less compassion fatigue, absenteeism and turnover
- Not having a damaging video show up on YouTube or the evening news

Our training is focused on the point of impact — the short period of time when disagreements, insults or gateway behaviors, such as swearing or aggressive posturing, can escalate to conflict and on to emotional and/or physical violence. We train "contact professionals" who directly interact with the general public or an organization's clients, and organizational teams who want to improve their performance by better managing conflict.

Vistelar's methodologies have been proven in real-world environments for over thirty years and are the subject of several books and training manuals in Vistelar's Confidence In Conflict and Conflict Management series[10].

Additional Information

We offer our training via speaking engagements, workshops, and instructor schools — using both live and online methods of instruction.

Our vision is to make the world safer by teaching everyone how to treat each other with dignity by showing respect.

Origins of Vistelar

The origins of Vistelar date back to the early 1980s when Gary T. Klugiewicz, a nationally known defensive tactics trainer and future co-founder of Vistelar, helped originate Wisconsin's "unified tactical training" systems (DAAT, P.O.S.C.®).

Since the mid-80s, every police officer, jail/juvenile detention officer and prison probation/parole officer is trained in these systems. In the mid-90s, he helped developed Professional Communications Skills (PCS), the communications component of Wisconsin's training system.

Gary T. Klugiewicz

Over the last three decades, Gary has implemented this unified tactical training system in scores of law enforcement agencies, correctional institutions and healthcare/mental health organizations throughout the United States. He also has been a national instructor for Calibre Press's Street Survival Seminar®, Team One Network, Redman Protective Gear and PoliceOne. Gary retired from the Milwaukee County Sheriff's Department in 2001 after 25 years in service.

In 1992, Gary started working closely with Dave Young, a nationally recognized defensive tactics trainer of law enforcement, corrections and the military. Gary and Dave worked together for over 17 years before founding Vistelar in 2009.

Dave Young

During this time, Gary and Dave worked with PoliceOne, ILEETA, and Force Science Research, and collaborated with many subject matter experts in the field of law enforcement and healthcare training, such as Robert Lindsey, Daniel Vega, Dr. Kevin Parsons, Charles Remsberg, Bob Willis, Col. Dave Grossman, Jack Hoban, Joel Lashley, and Jeff Mehring.

Allen Oelschlaeger

Vistelar was founded to enable Gary and Dave to disseminate their comprehensive training programs — that *address the entire spectrum of human conflict* — to a wider range of markets, including law enforcement, healthcare, loss prevention, security, education, hospitality, business, transit and corrections.

Since the founding of Vistelar by Gary, Dave and business executive, Allen Oelschlaeger, the company has extended its reach, published several books and manuals in its *Confidence In Conflict* series, introduced several conflict management online training programs, and greatly expanded its team of employees, trainers, advisors and certified instructors.

Today Vistelar is a world leader in point-of-impact conflict management training, which it offers as a comprehensive system of non-escalation and de-escalation coupled with physical alternatives.

To learn more:
   Call: 877-690-8230
   Email: info@vistelar.com
   Visit: www.vistelar.com

Additional Information

Acknowledgments

The authors would like to thank the many people who contributed to the subject matter of this manual over the span of the last 30+ years.

- Mike Delvaux — retired Captain, Wisconsin Department of Corrections
- Katie Dill — Vistelar Trainer
- Harry Dolan — retired Chief, Raleigh Police Department
- Jane Dresser — Director, Medical-Psychiatric Nursing Consultants, Inc.
- Andrew Garrison — President, BodyFacts Wellness Services
- Peter Harrell, Jr. — President, Harrell Communications
- Jack Hoban — President, Resolution Group International
- Peter Jaskulski — retired Captain, Milwaukee County Sheriff's Department
- Joel Lashley — Security Supervisor, Aurora Healthcare
- Chan Lee — Owner, J.K. Lee Black Belt Academy
- Robert Lindsey — retired Colonel, Jefferson Parish Sheriff's Office
- Gary Loop — President, Loop Group, LLC
- Jeff Mehring — retired Regional Director of Safety and Security, Wheaton-Franciscan Healthcare
- Dennis Nourse — Director, Mediation Center of Waukesha County
- Tony Pinelle — retired Chief, Public Safety Colorado Mental Health
- Joe Potterton — Security Operations Manager, The Children's Hospital of Philadelphia
- Vince Rampulla — VP Loss Prevention and Security, Roundy's Supermarkets, Inc.
- Charles Remsberg and Dennis Anderson — Founders, Calibre Press
- Dick Sem — President, Sem Security Management
- William Singleton — Partner, Vistelar
- Anthony Sherman — President, Genesis Group RMS
- Karen Stentz Huebner, PhD. — President, Purposeful Development Associates
- Kati Tillema — Partner, Vistelar
- Pablo Velazquez — Vistelar Trainer
- Daniel Vega, M.S.W. — Crisis Intervention Specialist, Tacoma, WA
- Derick Washington, Sr. — retired Lieutenant, Milwaukee County Sheriff's Office
- Jill Weisensel — Lieutenant, Marquette University Police Department
- Robert Whiteside — Executive Director, Security Mission Health
- Robert Willis — formerly Street Survival Instructor, Northeast Wisconsin Technical College
- Debbie Zwicky — Vistelar Trainer

Endnotes

[1] Alper, S., Tjosvold, D., & Law, K.S. (2000). Conflict Management, Efficacy, and Performance in Organizational Teams. *Personnel Psychology*. Vol 53, Issue 3, pp. 625-642

[2] DeChurch, L.A. & Marks, M.A. (2001). Maximizing the Benefits of Task Conflict: The Role of Conflict Management. *The International Journal of Conflict Management*. Vol. 12, No. 1, pp. 4-22

Amason, A.C. (1996). Distinguishing the effects of functional and dysfunctional conflict on strategic decision making: Resolving a paradox for top management teams. *Academy of Management Journal*, 39, pp.123–148

[3] "A small percentage of officers account for a disproportionate percentage of total citizen complaints. Excessive force and discourtesy were often the most common allegations lodged, and younger officers and those with less experience generally received a greater number of complaints. Providing those officers with appropriate training in empathy, professionalism, and de-escalation can help reduce those complaints."

Terell, W. & Ingram, J.R. (2016). Citizen Complaints Against the Police: An Eight City Examination. *Police Quarterly*. Vol. 19(2) pp. 150–179

[4] Research shows that, when it comes to customer service and organizational trust, people generally choose the organization with the better reputation. Additionally, those surveys show people have the least satisfaction with companies that fail to acknowledge the bad thing that happened and fail to try and make it right. Conflict management training equip people to do all of the above: build and protect the organizational reputation and culture, acknowledge missteps, and verbally de-escalate and repair them.

Bettenhausen K.L. (1991). Five years of groups research: What we have learned and what needs to be addressed. *Journal of Management*, 17, pp. 345–381

Bettenhausen K.L & Murnighan J.K. (1991). The development of an intragroup norm and the effects of interpersonal and structural challenges. *Administrative Science Quarterly*, 36, pp. 20–35

[5] Alper, S., Tjosvold, D., & Law, K.S. (2000). Conflict Management, Efficacy, and Performance in Organizational Teams. *Personnel Psychology*. Vol. 53, Issue 3, pp. 625–642

[6] Alper, S., Tjosvold, D., & Law, K.S. (2000). Conflict Management, Efficacy, and Performance in Organizational Teams. *Personnel Psychology*. Vol. 53, Issue 3, pp. 625–642

[7] Greenwald, A.G. and Krieger L.H. (2006) *Implicit Bias: Scientific Foundations*, 94 Cal. L. Rev. 945

[8] Yudkin, Daniel & Rothmund, Tobias & Twardawski, Mathias & Thalla, Natasha & J Van Bavel, Jay. (2016). Reflexive Intergroup Bias in Third-Party Punishment. *Journal of Experimental Psychology General*. pp. 145

[9] Huntington, B., & Kuhn, N. (2003). Communication gaffes: A root cause of malpractice claims. *Baylor University Medical Centre Proceedings*, 16(2), pp.157-161

Additional Information

Matsumoto, D., Frank, M.G., & Hwang, H. S. *Nonverbal Communication: Science and Applications.* Los Angeles: Sage Publications Inc., 2012.

[10] Matsumoto, D., Frank, M.G., & Hwang, H. S. *Nonverbal Communication: Science and Applications.* Sage Publications Inc., 2012.

Maccario, C. J. (2012). Aviation Security and Nonverbal Behavior. In *Nonverbal Communication: Science and Applications* (pp. 147-154)

Bibliography

De Becker, Gavin. *The Gift of Fear and Other Survival Signals that Protect Us From Violence*. Dell, 1999.

Elgin, Suzette Haden. *The Gentle Art of Verbal Self-Defense at Work*. Prentice Hall, 2000.

Fehr, B. J., & Exline, R. V. Social visual interactions: A conceptual and literature review. A.W. Siegman & S. Feldstein (Editors), *Nonverbal Behavior and Communication*, Psychology Press, 1987, pp. 225-326

Frank, M. G. & Eckman, P. (1997). The ability to detect deceit generalizes across different types of high-stake lies. *Journal of Personality and Social Psychology*, 72, 1429-1439

Hall, E. T. (1963). A system for the notation of proxemic behaviors. *American Anthropologist*, 65, 1003-1026

Hoban, Jack E. *The Ethical Warrior: Values, Morals and Ethics - For Life, Work and Service*. CreateSpace, 2012.

Huntington, B., & Kuhn, N. (2003). Communication gaffes: A root cause of malpractice claims. *Baylor University Medical Centre Proceedings*, 16(2), 157-161

Knapp, M. L., & Hall, J. A. *Nonverbal Communication in Human Interaction*. Wadsworth Publishing, 2013.

Gilmartin, Kevin, M. *Emotional survival for law enforcement: A guide for officers and their families*. E-S Press, 2002.

Grossman, Dave. *On Killing: The Psychological Cost of Learning to Kill in War and Society*. Back Bay Books, 2009.

Horn, Sam. *Tongue Fu!: How to Deflect, Disarm, and Defuse Any Verbal Conflict*. St. Martin's Griffin, 1997.

Katz, Neil H. et. al. *Communication & Conflict Resolution Skills*. Kendall Hunt Publishing, 1992.

Klugiewicz, Gary et. al. *Conflict Management For Law Enforcement*. Truths Publishing, 2016.

Lashley, Joel. *Confidence In Conflict For Healthcare Professionals: Creating an Environment of Care that is Incompatible with Violence*. Truths Publishing, 2015.

Jaskulski, Pete. *Confidence in Conflict for Sports Officials: Practical Tips for Staying Out of the Cross Fire and Keeping Peace During the Game*. Truths Publishing, 2015.

Mangold, Kathy. *Confidence In Conflict For Everyday Life: How to Prevent and Manage the Inevitable Conflict in Your Work and Personal Life*. Truths Publishing, 2014.

Matsumoto, D., Frank, M.G., & Hwang, H. S. *Nonverbal Communication: Science and Applications*. Sage Publications Inc., 2012.

Remsberg, Charles et. al. *Street Survival: Tactics For Armed Encounters*. Calibre Press, 1987.

Additional Information

Weisensel, Jill. *Confidence In Conflict For Campus Life: The Must-Have Safety Resource for Every College and College-Bound Student.* Truths Publishing, 2014.

Young, Dave. *How to Defend Your Family and Home: Outsmart an Invader, Secure Your Home, Prevent a Burglary and Protect Your Loved Ones from Any Threat.* Page Street Publishing, 2017.

Printed in Poland
by Amazon Fulfillment
Poland Sp. z o.o., Wrocław